SMART GUIDE®

CRE▲TIVE
HOMEOWNER®

W9-BOB-256

pruning

CREATIVE HOMEOWNER®, Upper Saddle River, New Jersey

SMART GUIDE: PRUNING

TECHNICAL EDITOR	Miranda Smith
SENIOR GRAPHIC DESIGN COORDINATOR	Glee Barre
DESIGNERS	Kathryn Wityk, David Geer
JUNIOR EDITOR	Jennifer Calvert
DIGITAL IMAGING SPECIALIST	Frank Dyer
INDEXER	Schroeder Indexing Services
FRONT COVER PHOTOGRAPHY	Neil Soderstrom
SMART GUIDE® SERIES COVER DESIGN	Clarke Barre
ILLUSTRATORS	Mavis Torke, Michele Angle Farrar, Todd Ferris

CREATIVE HOMEOWNER

VICE PRESIDENT AND PUBLISHER	Timothy O. Bakke
ART DIRECTOR	David Geer
MANAGING EDITOR	Fran J. Donegan
PRODUCTION COORDINATOR	Sara M. Markowitz

Current Printing (last digit)
10 9 8 7 6 5 4 3 2

Manufactured in the United States of America

Smart Guide®: Pruning, First Edition
Library of Congress Control Number: 2008935712
ISBN-10: 1-58011-444-X
ISBN-13: 978-1-58011-444-8

CREATIVE HOMEOWNER®
A Division of Federal Marketing Corp.
24 Park Way
Upper Saddle River, NJ 07458
www.creativehomeowner.com

Metric Conversion

Length

1 inch	25.4 mm
1 foot	0.3048 m
1 yard	0.9144 m
1 mile	1.61 km

Area

1 square inch	645 mm^2
1 square foot	0.0929 m^2
1 square yard	0.8361 m^2
1 acre	4046.86 m^2
1 square mile	2.59 km^2

Volume

1 cubic inch	16.3870 cm^3
1 cubic foot	0.03 m^3
1 cubic yard	0.77 m^3

Common Lumber Equivalents

Sizes: Metric cross sections are so close to their U.S. sizes, as noted below, that for most purposes they may be considered equivalents.

Dimensional lumber	1 x 2	19 x 38 mm
	1 x 4	19 x 89 mm
	2 x 2	38 x 38 mm
	2 x 4	38 x 89 mm
	2 x 6	38 x 140 mm
	2 x 8	38 x 184 mm
	2 x 10	38 x 235 mm
	2 x 12	38 x 286 mm
Sheet sizes	4 x 8 ft.	1200 x 2400 mm
	4 x 10 ft.	1200 x 3000 mm
Sheet thicknesses	¼ in.	6 mm
	⅜ in.	9 mm
	½ in.	12 mm
	¾ in.	19 mm
Stud/joist spacing	16 in. o.c.	400 mm o.c.
	24 in. o.c.	600 mm o.c.

Capacity

1 fluid ounce	29.57 mL
1 pint	473.18 mL
1 quart	1.14 L
1 gallon	3.79 L

Weight

1 ounce	28.35g
1 pound	0.45kg

Temperature

Celsius = Fahrenheit − 32 x $\frac{5}{9}$

Fahrenheit = Celsius x 1.8 + 32

contents

safety first

All projects and procedures in this book have been reviewed for safety; still it is not possible to overstate the importance of working carefully. What follows are reminders for plant care and project safety. Always use common sense.

- *Always* use caution, care, and good judgment when following the procedures in this book.

- *Always* determine locations of underground utility lines before you dig, and then avoid them by a safe distance. Buried lines may be for gas, electricity, communications, or water. Contact local utility companies who will help you map their lines.

- *Always* read and heed tool manufacturer instructions.

- *Always* ensure that the electrical setup is safe; be sure that no circuit is overloaded and that all power tools and electrical outlets are properly grounded and protected by a ground-fault circuit interrupter (GCFI). Do not use power tools in wet locations.

- *Always* wear eye protection when using chemicals, sawing wood, pruning trees and shrubs, using power tools, and striking metal onto metal or concrete.

- *Always* consider nontoxic and least toxic methods of addressing unwanted plants, plant pests, and plant diseases before resorting to toxic methods. Follow package application and safety instructions carefully.

- *Always* read labels on chemicals, solvents, and other products; provide ventilation; heed warnings.

- *Always* wear a hard hat when working in situations with potential for injury from falling tree limbs.

- *Always* wear appropriate gloves in situations in which your hands could be injured by rough surfaces, sharp edges, thorns, or poisonous plants.

- *Always* protect yourself against ticks, which can carry Lyme disease. Wear light-colored, long-sleeved shirts and pants. Inspect yourself for ticks after every session in the garden.

- *Always* wear a disposable face mask or a special filtering respirator when creating sawdust or working with toxic gardening substances.

- *Always* keep your hands and other body parts away from the business end of blades, cutters, and bits.

- *Always* obtain approval from local building officials before undertaking construction of permanent structures.

- *Never* employ herbicides, pesticides, or toxic chemicals unless you have determined with certainty that they were developed for the specific problem you hope to remedy.

- *Never* allow bystanders to approach work areas where they might by injured by workers or work-site hazards. Be sure work areas are well marked.

- *Never* work with power tools when you are tired, or under the influence of alcohol or drugs.

- *Never* carry sharp or pointed tools, such as knives or saws, in your pocket.

introduction

Just Prune

Pruning is easier than you may imagine. Once you learn how plants respond to being pruned and understand that good pruning depends on matching the particular pruning task to both the type of plant you are pruning and the season, you can prune with confidence.

Smart Guide: Pruning teaches you how to make various cuts and explains how plants respond to them. You'll learn which tools to use and how to time your work so that the pruning you do is most effective and the plant remains healthy and productive. Additionally, the plant directories in each section of the guide, which cover shrubs and perennials, roses, hedges, trees, and fruits, give instructions for pruning literally hundreds of plants.

Beyond this, begin slowly. Install plants that require very little pruning, and get used to shaping and trimming them before you embark on more challenging projects such as fruit trees or topiary art. Eventually, pruning will seem as natural and straightforward as any other job in the garden. When that happens, you'll know you have become a real pruner.

chapter 1
about pruning

Pruning Basics

Skillful pruning is a real pleasure. It keeps your plants healthy, increases the numbers and beauty of flowers and fruits, and adds to the beauty of your home landscape. And best of all, it's much easier than you might imagine!

If you are a beginning pruner, you may think that it's going to take so much time and effort to master that you'd rather grow plants that don't need pruning or "let nature take its course" and allow the plants to "prune themselves."

But the only plants that don't need pruning are annuals—and as soon as you pluck off a single faded flower, you're pruning. So you can't really say that most annuals don't need pruning. And if you want diversity in your yard and gardens—shade trees, perennial flowers, maybe some fruits—everything will perform a lot better with some pruning.

Natural Pruning. Nature does prune plants, of course. But nature doesn't try to keep the plants in your yard healthy and productive. Instead, nature works on the level of the big picture, providing niches for all organisms. For example, a storm may tear off part of a branch from a tree, leaving a lot of the interior exposed. Huge numbers of pests and disease organisms that feed on both living and dead wood can then assault it, and nature is well served. But the tree is likely to suffer a shortened, sickly life. If you had pruned off the vulnerable branch before the storm or, in the worst case scenario, tidied it up afterwards, the tree would have been spared.

There are four important things to learn about pruning any plant:
• WHY to prune it—if you have a purpose in mind, you'll be able to prune intelligently.
• WHEN to prune it—different plants have different requirements,

Espaliered trees add a note of elegance to any yard.

Improve Plant Health by
- removing dead, diseased, and crowded growth.
- decreasing the incidence of diseases that thrive in low light and stagnant air.
- removing poorly positioned branches that are vulnerable in storms.

Improve Plant Productivity by
- removing excess buds or fruit, which stimulates remaining ones to reach their full potential.
- removing excess branches to allow remaining ones to grow vigorously.
- allowing sunlight into the plant and to ripen fruit.

Improve Plant Beauty by
- keeping plants in their allotted areas.
- creating pleasing forms.
- creating plant vigor, making plants more beautiful.

and sometimes different timing gives different results.
• WHERE to prune it—you sometimes remove a whole branch or limb and sometimes just cut off a few inches of a branch or even just the tip.
• And finally, HOW to prune it—

using the right tools results in clean cuts that heal quickly.

Fortunately, once you learn the simple techniques presented in the following pages, you'll understand why experienced gardeners look forward to their pruning tasks.

Tools are vitally important when it comes to pruning. The right tool allows you to accomplish all of your pruning quickly and efficiently. However, using the wrong one will be as frustrating as trying to slice through a raw beet with a butter knife.

As you look at the illustrations on the next few pages, you're likely to feel overwhelmed. Chances are, at least a part of why you got into gardening in the first place was to save money, not to spend a bundle on new tools! So what you do really need?

To a large extent, what you need depends on what you are growing. But some tools are universal. **Good pruning shears** top the list—you'll use them for more things than you can imagine. If you budget for only one pair, choose **bypass shears** because the shape of their blades makes cleaner cuts, thus they are more versatile than anvil shears.

When plants are small, a **folding pull saw** is adequate. However, once your trees have grown, your needs for a **bow and/or pole saw** will also have grown. And if you've inherited plants you need to bring back to vitality, you'll also need larger tools.

Long loppers are essential if you're reaching in to remove old bramble canes because you can get at the cane without subjecting yourself to the thorns in the middle of the bush. They also allow you to prune in spots you couldn't otherwise reach, and the racheting action on some loppers increases your cutting power without stressing the tool.

Hedge shears are required only if you have a hedge. Manual ones are fine up to about 20 feet of hedging. Beyond that, you might want to buy **electric shears**— unless you are willing to devote a couple of weekends a year to trimming the hedge.

Hand-Pruning Tools

Price is often a reliable gauge of tool quality. Still, some modestly priced tools can give a lifetime of service if you treat them well. Keep blades sharp, and oil joints periodically. After use, wipe dirt from blades, and remove sap using a solvent such as kerosene. Store tools in a dry place, safely away from children. To prevent rust, oil all metal before long-term storage.

Pastured cattle can keep conifers looking compact because they nibble only the young new shoots each spring, sparing the less tender older growth. So too can **hand pruning** keep growth of conifers and broad-leaved evergreens in check.

Folding pruning knives are handy for a range of tasks, from cutting wood to severing twine.

Bypass shears   Anvil shears

Bypass pruning shears employ two curved blades consisting of a cutting blade that passes close by a flat-edged branch-gripping blade. Springs reopen the blade effortlessly for the user. For cleanest cuts at branch crotches, position the blade nearer the collar of the limb you wish to save. Bypass shears are designed for wood up to about ½ inch in diameter, as are anvil shears.

Anvil pruning shears employ a straight cutting blade that presses against the flat surface of a mating anvil-like blade. These shears provide good cutting force relative to exertion. The cutting blade stops at the anvil. However, anvil shears tend to crush stems and don't allow the precise close fit in branch crotches that bypass pruners do, and their anvils almost always damage branch collars.

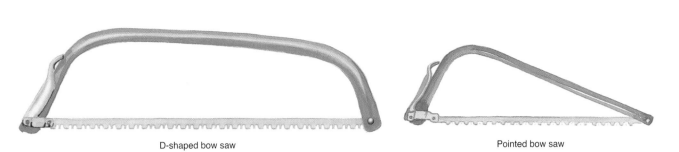

D-shaped bow saw

Pointed bow saw

Bow saws equipped with high-quality blades make quick work of limbs up to several inches in diameter. The position of the handle, above the line of the blade, allows forceful thrusts on the push stroke. The pointed bow saw allows cutting in tight quarters but can limit depth of cut. D-shaped bow saws come in lengths from 21 to more than 40 inches, allowing deeper cuts and even two-person sawing.

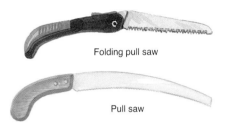

Folding pull saw

Pull saw

Pull saws, also known as Grecian saws, cut on the pull stroke. They are great in tight quarters and easy to use overhead. Folding versions can be safely carried in a pocket. Fixed-blade saws are more safely transported in specially designed scabbards.

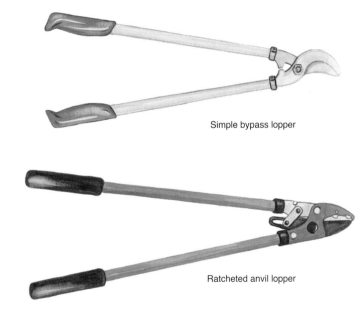

Simple bypass lopper

Ratcheted anvil lopper

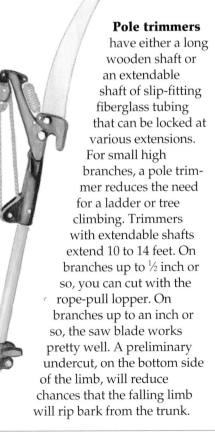

Pole trimmers have either a long wooden shaft or an extendable shaft of slip-fitting fiberglass tubing that can be locked at various extensions. For small high branches, a pole trimmer reduces the need for a ladder or tree climbing. Trimmers with extendable shafts extend 10 to 14 feet. On branches up to ½ inch or so, you can cut with the rope-pull lopper. On branches up to an inch or so, the saw blade works pretty well. A preliminary undercut, on the bottom side of the limb, will reduce chances that the falling limb will rip bark from the trunk.

Loppers are essentially heftier variations of bypass and anvil pruning shears. They require two-hand operation and can cut larger branches. They are especially handy for pruning in hard-to-reach places. The bigger loppers have ratchet mechanisms that increase cutting force without increasing cutting effort. Some models can handle branches up to 1½ inches in diameter. Whatever your lopper size and design, use it only on limbs and saplings that fit deeply into the cutting jaws, allowing maximum cutting efficiency without overtaxing stress points. The leverage provided by long handles encourages strong people to overtax their lopper, which can break or bend handles and blade assemblies.

Shears

In skilled hands, **manual hedge shears** can handle the range of tasks from light flat trims to elaborate curves of topiary. The challenge is to eyeball smooth cutting planes while your hands and arms perform a choppy operation.

Electric hedge shears allow smooth, low-effort trimming as you gracefully sweep the tool over intended planes. For best control of the power-cord extension, drape it over the shoulder on the side of your direction of travel.

Power Pruners

Safety Note: for all electric tools, be sure your extension cable meets manufacturer's specifications and that it is protected by a ground-fault circuit interrupter (GFCI).

A reciprocating saw can be an excellent pruner, especially when you need to annually cut near ground level about a third of the stems in a row of lilacs.

Chain saws are available in electric or gas-powered models. You may not need a chain saw for general pruning, unless you plan to make a lot of firewood on an annual basis. For occasional trees with trunks less than 4 inches in diameter, a bow saw can be an efficient alternative. However, if you need a chain saw and can do most cutting within 100 feet of an outdoor outlet, an electric chain saw is probably all you'll need.

In contrast to bigger, heavier gas-powered chain saws, electrics emit no exhaust fumes and are low maintenance, low cost, and quieter. They are always ready to go. As with a gas-powered saw, the chain needs sharpening whenever it begins to show signs of dulling.

A dull chain produces sawdust-size particles and cuts so slowly that it tempts you to mistakenly apply more pressure to the bar. A sharp chain yields wood chips the size of dry oatmeal and cuts through wood almost as though it were butter. Low-cost sharpening jigs mount on the saw bar and allow you to sharpen each cutter at the same precise angle and depth.

Caution: A chain saw is one of the most dangerous power tools in common use, particularly in the hands of inexperienced, fatigued, or careless people. The prime single hazard is deep bone-cutting injury resulting from saw kickback, which can occur when the chain arcing around the nose of the bar unexpectedly hits resistance, such as an unnoticed limb or other obstruction. To avoid kickback, always hold the saw by both handles with a firm opposable-thumb grip and with your left elbow extended, not bent. At the very least, study the manufacturer's owner's manual and heed all its safety instructions.

Pruning Techniques

Although pruning techniques differ according to the type, size, and shape of the plant, most of them are based on one procedure—cutting. And the way you cut is vitally important because plants heal most quickly if a cut is clean, with no ragged edges or torn bark. To produce this kind of cut, always use the appropriate tool, and sharpen it before pruning.

The best attitude when cutting is similar to the way you approach cutting in the kitchen or the workshop. Once you have determined where to cut, do it with conviction. Changing your mind mid-cut or feeling tentative often results in a cut with ragged edges. If that happens, you can always clean it up, but it's best to avoid the problem. So if possible, practice on weedy plants in the woods before beginning to prune in your own yard.

Good observational skills are also worth cultivating. As you'll learn in the following pages, you must know when plants bloom to prune them correctly, so you will have to watch them. You'll also have to come to know your individual plants and observe how they respond to pruning.

Plant Behavior. Plants always try to revert to their natural shape and size, which is partially determined by plant compounds called "auxins." For example, many plants display "apical dominance," meaning that their topmost growth releases an auxin that inhibits the growth of buds further down on the branch. When you prune off the top, and the site of the auxin production, lower buds have a chance to develop. But before long, one or two of them will be releasing that same auxin and lower buds will be inhibited again. Also, when young, plants tend to grow quickly and upwards rather than to the sides. This is the time you must prune to help the plant develop the strongest and most productive framework possible. When the plant gets older, growth slows. Though you'll still need to do some pruning, it won't be nearly as much or as urgent.

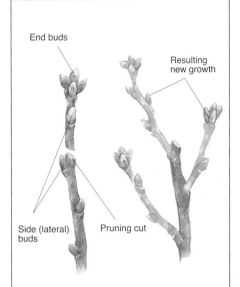

End buds

Resulting new growth

Side (lateral) buds

Pruning cut

Removing an end bud or shoot will stimulate dormant buds below it to grow, producing side shoots and creating a bushier plant. If you allow end buds to remain, they will actually inhibit the growth of side buds, and the stem will continue to grow mainly from the tip.

To prune branches with alternate buds, find a bud pointing in the direction you want your branch to grow. Make your cut about ¼ in. above the bud and on an angle parallel with that bud. There is no need to apply tree wound dressing to cuts, whether small or large.

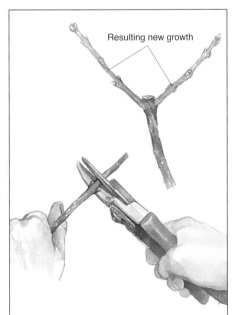

Resulting new growth

To prune branches with opposite buds, such as those of maple and ash, cut straight across in a line that just clears the bud tips. This will result in the fairly uniform growth of both buds.

When pruning with a lopper or with pruning shears, place the blade side nearer the part you wish to save. Cut just outside the branch collar at the angle shown. This will help you avoid leaving a stub.

Shaping

Shaping a plant depends on working with its basic nature. You cannot turn an avocado tree into a multi-stemmed bush, for example, or a forsythia bush into a tree with just one trunk. However, you can do a lot with the natural form of a bush simply by following the rules of its growth pattern, as shown in the illustrations on the previous page. By cutting so the top bud faces away from the center of the plant, you can open the plant up and increase both light penetration and air circulation. Conversely, by cutting so the top bud faces inward, you can make the bush denser. Step back and visualize the likely results of your pruning before you make a cut.

While not absolutely foolproof, the following tricks work most of the time. If you want to stimulate a particular bud to grow, cut a notch into the wood just above the bud right before the plant is about to break dormancy. This notch prevents the inhibiting auxin that the branch tip is sending down from reaching that bud.

The opposite is usually true, too. If you cut a notch just below the bud, it will not develop or, if it does, its growth will be extremely slow.

Sanitation

Diseased wood is often removed by pruning. With many diseases, this simple remedy solves the problem—the diseased wood is cut out and removed, and healthy wood remains to continue growing.

However, you can also spread a disease by pruning. A few stray bacteria may hitch a ride on the pruning shears from one place on the plant to another or even to a different plant. Avoid this by dipping the blades in a 10 percent laundry bleach solution (1 part bleach to 9 parts water) before and between every cut.

Shaping Plants for Growth

Leggy growth without pinching

Lush, bushy growth after a program of pinching

Leaf bud

Flower bud

Pinching back broad-leaved evergreens, such as rhododendrons, encourages them to grow more thickly. The plant on the left is leggy because it wasn't pinched back, while the one on the right is more dense and attractive. Balance your desire for lush growth with the need for good air circulation, though. Remember to leave enough space between branches so air can easily flow through the plant. To make the plant just a little more dense, remove only the leaf buds. Leave the fatter flower buds in place so you'll have blooms when spring arrives.

When to Prune

Pruning stimulates growth in woody plants—just as deadheading and pinching back stimulate flower and foliage production in herbaceous plants. This basic principle, combined with the blooming period of flowering plants, governs the pruning timetables below.

In general, drastic hard pruning shortly before the growing season promotes the most growth; light pruning or late-season pruning encourages less vigorous growth. Avoid pruning after midsummer before the onset of dormancy; pruning at that time can damage a plant by causing a spurt of tender new growth that may not have time to harden enough to withstand winter's cold.

Evergreens
In spring, prune
- winter and snow damage before active growth begins.
- pines, firs, spruces, and other conifers to encourage dense branching and improve shape by shearing the light green new growth in early spring. Cut off the tips or half the new growth of pine shoots, or candles.
- new growth once or twice more at intervals of a week to slow or dwarf the development of coniferous evergreens. This will also help avoid unsightly cuts.
- plants that bloom on new wood (many of which flower in summer). To encourage flowering, prune old wood in late winter or early spring before growth begins.
- no more than one-third of the total green foliage in one season to renovate overgrown broad-leaved shrubs.

In summer, prune
- plants that bloom on old wood (many of which bloom in spring). Prune just after the flowers have faded; then let the plants grow new branches and flower buds that will bloom the following season.
- to shape or slow the growth of broad-leaved evergreens. Prune in early summer, after flowering. Prune hollies in mid- to late summer.

In fall and winter, prune
- coniferous evergreens when removing branches to correct shape or thin congested growth.
- lightly for holiday greens. (This won't harm the plants.)

Any time, prune
- dead, damaged, or diseased branches.
- lightly for decorative greens and flowers.

Deciduous Trees and Shrubs
In spring, prune
- plants that bloom on new wood (many of which flower in summer). Prune before new growth begins, in late winter or early spring, to promote flowering.

In summer, prune
- plants that bloom on old wood (many of which flower in spring). Prune immediately after the blooms fade to avoid cutting off newly formed flower buds and to stimulate growth of more buds for next year's bloom.
- young foliage plants (in early summer) to encourage dense branching. Cut back by half the succulent stems that are beginning to grow lateral shoots.
- to slow or dwarf growth in summer after the seasonal growth is complete.
- to control height when plants have reached the desired size, after the new growth has fully developed. (Extend the cuts back a bit into old wood.)
- trees that bleed, such as maples and birches.

In fall and winter, prune
- to shape and train trees when dormant.
- to renovate overgrown shrubs when dormant.

Any time, prune
- dead, diseased, or damaged wood. (Prune dead wood before leaves fall; otherwise you may have a hard time distinguishing it from dormant wood.)
- lightly, for indoor use as decorative greens, flowers, and winter branches.

chapter 2

pruning perennials & shrubs

Pruning Shrubs

Shrubs and perennials require very similar pruning techniques. You'll find that the differences are only a matter of degree—shrubs, because of their greater size, need more pruning attention than most perennials, but other than that, pruning techniques are the same.

Pinching

Pinching is as simple as literally pinching off the soft growth at the tip of a stem. With clean hands on healthy plants, simply grasp a stem tip between your forefinger and thumbnail, and sharply pinch off the top growth. But if the plant shows any signs of disease, use a pair of bypass pruning shears, and sterilize the blades between cuts.

Depending on how densely you want the plant to grow, you can pinch off the growing tips of the subsequent new shoots after they have two or three sets of leaves or wait until they are five or six inches long. Every time you pinch, you'll be stimulating the growth of new branches.

Plants that respond especially well to pinching include branching annuals as well as many perennials. For example, fuchsias, coleus, and zonal geraniums (*Pelargonium* spp.) have a tendency to grow quite leggy unless they are in bright light. Pinch off the growing tips regularly to create a plant with many branches.

Branching perennials, including such plants as yarrows (*Achillea* spp.), columbines (*Aquilegia*), *Artemisia* species, asters, chrysanthemums, and coreopsis, true geraniums, hibiscus, beardtongue (*Penstemon barbatus*), Russian sage, and (*Perovskia atriplicifolia*), black–eyed Susans (*Rudbeckia* spp.), salvias, goldenrods (*Solidiago* spp.), and veronicas, all respond well to pinching. But don't confine yourself to this list. If you have a branching plant—as opposed to a bulbous one—such as an oriental lily, or a rosette forming one such as lamb's ears (*Stachys byzantina*), and it is growing too long and leggy, pinch off a couple of stem tips and see how it responds.

Pinching Plants

To encourage a bushier, fuller form in perennials with a branched habit of growth, pinch off the growing tips of the young plants. Pinch off the tip of each stem to the next set of leaves. A new shoot will grow in each leaf axil, giving you two branches in the place of one. To make the plant even bushier, pinch the tips of these secondary shoots after they develop.

Disbudding

Disbudding, as shown above right, is often done to plants being grown for exhibition blooms. When all but one flower bud is removed from a cluster, the bloom it grows will become much larger than normal. Dahlias, chrysanthemums, peonies, and carnations are often disbudded.

Commercial tomato growers also disbud to produce a different effect. They remove the single terminal flower of a cluster. This "king blossom" generally produces a larger fruit than the other flowers, so removing it gives a more uniform crop that is easier to ship. Some commercial flower growers do this, too. Removing the top bud on a plant stimulates the plant to produce more side buds. If you decide to practice either form of disbudding, do it before the buds get very large, otherwise, your effort will be wasted.

Thinning

Thinning is the term used for removing an entire branch or cane, generally just above the soil surface. On woody shrubs and perennials, it

Disbudding

Chrysanthemums are one of the plants that most benefit from pinching; a well-branched plant will produce many blooms. But if you want to grow exhibition-size mums, you want the plant to produce fewer, larger flowers. To get larger flowers, pinch off—or disbud—all but the side shoots from the main stems, and when flower buds form, remove all but one or two from each stem.

These Siberian irises are ready for cutting back in fall.

increases the air circulation between the stems, improves their appearance, and also increases the size of the remaining blooms. Plants that respond particularly well to being thinned include all the bramble fruit (*Rubus* spp.), such as raspberries and blackberries, asters, delphiniums, bee balm (*Monarda didyma*), and phlox (*Phlox paniculata*).

Pruning Shrubs

Pruning your shrubs to keep them healthy and productive is no more difficult than pruning perennials. But for the best results, it's wise to pay attention to a few details.

When you buy a shrub, it may be either containerized or bare root, meaning that there is no soil around the root. In either case, the roots may need some "pruning" before you plant. If it is bare root, examine the roots and cut off any that look dead or damaged. If it's in a container, you'll have to encourage the roots to grow outwards rather than in a tight little circle. As shown below, cut into the rootball, and pull out some of the roots. You'll need to do this to a greater extent on plants whose roots are obviously circling the pot, but take care to leave enough roots to support the plant while it's getting established.

Look at the top growth, too. Prune off any dead or damaged branches. Otherwise, leave the top growth alone until the plant is well established. Once you can see that the roots are growing nicely into the surrounding soil and the plant is putting on new, healthy growth, prune out any branches that cross each other; thin or prune off weak branches; and cut back the tips of straggly growth.

As shrubs grow, prune them only as necessary to shape them and keep them healthy, paying attention to their individual needs. To create a thicker, more bushy plant, cut back new shoots by about half. If they have alternate leaves, remember to cut to an outward facing bud to avoid creating crowded conditions in the center of the plant. If the leaves are opposite, place the cut where you want new branches to develop.

As shown in the illustrations opposite, timing is also imperative. For example, spring-blooming shrubs such as lilac bloom on "old" wood—the wood that grew the previous year. They require deadheading and thinning after they bloom. In contrast, late summer and fall-blooming plants flower on "new" wood. They are pruned in early spring and may benefit from a "hard pruning," meaning that they are cut back to a 1-foot-tall framework, as you do with Potentilla, or nearly to the ground, as you do with butterfly bush (*Buddleia davidii*). You'll find information about individual shrubs on pages 20–31.

Most of the routine cuts to your shrubs are easy to make with pruning shears or, if you need to reach into the center of the plant, long loopers. Loopers are also a good choice if the branch is woody or thick—their length gives you needed leverage. Hedges, which are discussed on pages 44–53, are usually pruned with hedge shears, although you can trim off stray growth with pruning shears if you catch it when it's young.

Circling roots here indicate that the plant is pot bound. Make at least 4 or 5 deep vertical cuts into the rootball before planting.

After making the vertical cuts, use your fingers to gently tease out some roots, and position them so they grow into the surrounding soil.

Vigorous growers, such as this butterfly bush (*Buddleia davidii*), need hard pruning, as evidenced by the new shoots growing from what look like dead branches.

Pruning when Dormant.
For plants that bloom on new wood (mostly summer bloomers, such as potentilla, abelia, and St. John's wort), prune when the plant is dormant. Prune all suckers, dead and broken wood, and taller, older branches. Your goal is to remove about one-third of the old wood each year, gradually replacing all wood over several years.

Plants that Bloom on New Wood

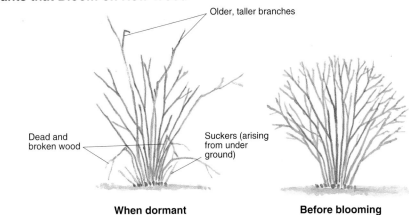

When dormant — Before blooming

(labels: Older, taller branches; Dead and broken wood; Suckers (arising from under ground))

Pruning after Flowering. Shrubs such as forsythia, lilac, and mock orange bloom on old wood (previous year's branches) in spring. After blooms have faded, prune out old, broken, and diseased wood. Then thin out about one-third of the taller, older branches close to ground level.

Forsythia

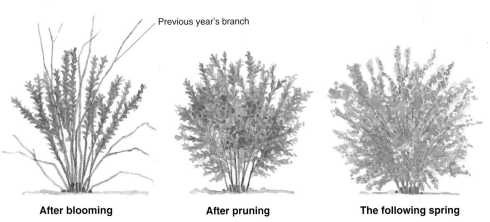

(label: Previous year's branch)

After blooming — After pruning — The following spring

Hard Pruning after Flowering (for a vigorous grower). Fast-growing shrubs that flower on old wood (mostly late spring and summer), such as spirea and weigela, often have overcrowded branches that can result in fewer flowers the next year and leave the plant looking unkempt. After flowering, prune hard to just above the new shoots.

Weigela

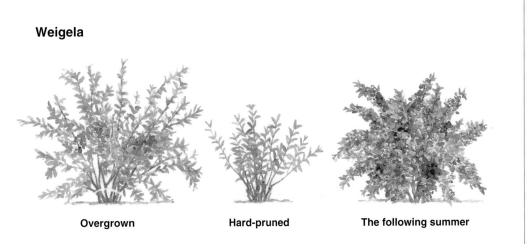

Overgrown — Hard-pruned — The following summer

Inherited Shrubs

One of the best things about moving into an older home is that you're likely to inherit established gardens and shrubbery. But this can be a mixed blessing, particularly if the previous owner grew a little sloppy about keeping up with pruning chores. If you inherit some overgrown, neglected shrubs, there are two courses of action that make sense: remove them or renovate them.

Examine the shrubs carefully before making your decision. If they are diseased, do a little research to discover the source of the problem. Some diseases, such as powdery mildew and leaf and flower galls, can be cured with the proper pruning to thin out crowded growth and the occasional application of a fungicide such as copper or zinc. If this is the case, renovation, as described at right, is your best course of action.

However, if the crown and roots of a shrub are suffering from a serious disease that causes them to rot, curing the problem may be more trouble than it would be worth or, more likely, nearly impossible to achieve. In this case, you'll want to remove the shrub entirely, taking as much of the soil surrounding the root ball as practical. Even if you remove what seems like an enormous amount of soil, it's rare to completely eradicate the disease organisms. If you plant a new shrub or tree in the area, these organisms may attack it, too. So play it safe by filling in the hole with fresh soil, mixed with fully finished compost, and planting grass or annuals there. Wait at least five or six years before planting another woody shrub or perennial there. If the spot simply demands a big plant, install a large, wheeled container filled with a dramatic specimen plant.

Renovating Shrubs

Renovation techniques differ according to the type of shrub. Most overgrown deciduous shrubs, including mock oranges, deutzias, and hydrangeas, respond well to heavy pruning, done all at once. But wait until the late winter or early spring. Thin out the dead or poorly positioned branches first by cutting them at ground level. Next, cut back the healthy branches you want to keep to within about a foot from the ground.

The plant will respond by sending up new shoots from the lower buds during the growing season. The following spring, thin out these branches to keep the center open. In subsequent years, prune as if the plant had never been neglected, paying attention to the proper timing according to the bloom time and any other requirements.

Coppicing. Some woody plants that have grown too large for their space can be cut back every year or two to within a few inches of the ground. The illustration above shows red-osier dogwood. New sprouts from the substantial root system will spring forth and can be selectively pruned into new forms.

Pinch back the branch tips on azaleas right after their blooms fade.

Fothergilla **species** bloom in early spring but are pruned in late winter when old or crowded growth is thinned out.

Dealing with Evergreens. Evergreens are handled somewhat differently. For one thing, many species do not grow sprouts from buds on old wood, so if you cut them back to nothing but old wood, they will die. Junipers, spruces, and pines are in this category. Look at the plant carefully before you prune, and take only the dead or diseased branches that need to be entirely removed. If you want to trim the plant to make it a more manageable size, wait until spring and cut back the tips of the developing growth. Pines are an exception; they can lose too much sap if pruned early. Instead, wait until late spring to cut them back.

Evergreens are also pruned according to their growth periods. Narrowleaf evergreens, including plants such as yew, juniper, and arborvitae, grow all through the year, and can be pruned every spring if necessary. In contrast, broadleaf evergreens, including shrubs such as rhododendrons, hollies (*Ilex* spp.), and mountain laurels (*Kalmia latifo-lia*), put on new growth only in the spring and are typically pruned only every two or three years. If you are renovating a broadleaf evergreen, do it gradually, because it will suffer if too much growth is removed at once. The first year, thin out dead, diseased, or poorly positioned branches, and cut back the remaining stems by half. The second year, cut back half the remaining old stems, and thin new growth if it is crowded. The third year, cut back the remaining old stems.

Special Effects

Training a Shrub Against a Wall. Some shrubs make good espalier plants. Many shrubs can be trained against a flat vertical surface.

Try quince, camellias, hollies, pyracanthas, roses, and other shrubs with flowers that develop along stems and that tolerate the hard pruning necessary to train them. If you have a structure to support it, an espalier is an ideal feature in a small garden, and the results are quick.

Training Evergreens as Topiary. The art of shaping plants, or *topiary,* has been practiced since the days of ancient Rome. Over the centuries, shrubs have been trained and carved into fantastic forms resembling animals, ships, or human figures. If you want to create a topiary, start with a simple geometric shape—a ball, cube, or cone—made of yew, arborvitae, or boxwood. You'll need to start trimming while the plant is young and keep snipping as it grows. Training a shrub into a standard, or single-trunk, form is easy. But you need to create that central trunk early.

Espalier training makes pyracantha an especially striking feature, whether informal, here, or formal.

This topiary rooster was fashioned from a boxwood. He's either riled up or due for another shearing.

Aucuba japonica

Gold-Dust Tree, Japanese Laurel
CORNACEAE

Variegated cultivars of this lovely, evergreen shrub brighten shady areas all through the year.

Hardiness Zones 7–10

Size 6 to 10 feet tall

Appearance These bushes are naturally upright and rounded in habit with dense growth. The stiff, elliptical leaves are from 3 to 8 inches long and are a dark green, with white or yellow variegations in many cultivars. Male and female flowers grow on different plants, so you'll need a male cultivar, such as 'Maculata', to fertilize female flowers. Fertilized female plants produce bright red berries in the fall.

Exposure Partial to full shade

Soil and Water Well-drained, high humus soil with moderate fertility and a wide pH range. Thrives in moist soil but also tolerates droughty periods.

Comments Variegated cultivars include 'Veriegata', with yellow markings, and 'Mr. Goldstrike', with bright yellow markings, that grows only 4 to 6 feet tall.

Gold-dust tree (*Aucuba japonica* 'Variegata')

Gold-dust tree (*Aucuba japonica* 'Variegata')

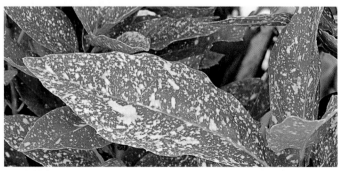

Gold-dust tree (*Aucuba japonica* 'Variegata')

Recommended Pruning

Season Early spring

Recommended Forms Informal bush

Shaping The natural form is elegant so you won't have to do more than cut out crowded or dead growth and cut back branches that threaten to elongate too much.

Maintaining Only cut back stems as necessary to allow good circulation in the center of the shrub.

Restoring Follow the directions on page 19 for restoring broadleaf evergreens over a period of three years.

Buddleia spp.

Butterfly bush
LOGANIACEAE

This deciduous, flowering shrub lives up to the promise of its common name. When it is in bloom, butterflies from miles around flock to feed on it.

Hardiness Zones 5–9

Size 6 to 8 feet tall, 3 to 6 feet wide

Appearance This naturally graceful shrub has elegantly arching branches that are tipped with 6 to 10-inch-long panicles of purple, pink, white, and red florets, often with an orange throat, that give off a honey-scented fragrance. The 4 to 10-inch-long leaves are gray to blue-green on top with hairy, silvery-looking undersides.

Alternate-leaf butterfly bush (*Buddleia alternifolia*)

Exposure Full sun

Soil and Water Plant in very well-drained soil with moderate fertility and an almost-neutral pH. Plants do not tolerate consistently wet soils.

Comments Give these beauties plenty of space to allow them to develop to their full potential. They are quite pest and disease-resistant, unless you allow them to become so crowded that air doesn't circulate freely around them.

Orange ball tree (*Buddleia globosa*)

Recommended Pruning

Season Late winter or very early spring. In summer, deadhead faded blooms for increased production.

Recommended Forms Informal bush

Shaping Butterfly bushes look best when allowed to assume their natural, arching form. Pinch or thin any crowded growth when you prune.

Maintaining Cut back all stems you want to retain to about a foot above the soil surface every year in late winter. To keep the plant vigorous, cut back about a third of the oldest branches starting in the fourth year from the time you planted it.

Restoring Cut the plant back in late winter, and thin out all the old and crowded branches.

Butterfly bush (*Buddleia davidii*)

Chaenomeles spp.

Flowering Quince
ROSACEAE

These early-blooming shrubs light up the spring land-scape with flowers that look like miniature roses.

Hardiness Zones 5–9

Size 3 to 8 feet tall, 6 to 15 feet wide

Appearance Leaves are mid-green, toothed, and glossy. Flowers are cup-shaped, single or double, and have the prominent center of all rose-family blooms. Colors include white and shades of pink and red. The flowers open just before or while the shrub is leafing out. Small, quince-like fruit that are often used in traditional Chinese medicine form in the fall.

Exposure Full sun or partial shade

Soil and Water Plant in well-drained, moderately fertile soil. They are tolerant of urban soils but suffer in alkaline ones.

Comments *C. speciosa* is the most common flowering quince. This shrub is very wide, and branches can get tangled if they aren't pruned. Favorite cultivars include 'Apple Blossom', which bears very large flowers that are white with a pink blush. 'Dwarf Orange' and 'Dwarf White' are both low-growing, only to 4 feet high, and spreading. Their names describe the colors of their flowers. 'Simonii' is a striking plant that has very large, blood-red flowers that are double.

    C. x *superba* is a cross between *C. japonica*, a 3-foot-tall species, and *C. speciosa*. It averages 5 feet high by 6 feet wide and is more rounded in habit than *C. speciosa*. 'Rowallane' is one of the most popular cultivars, perhaps because of its low, 3-foot growth and brilliant scarlet flowers. 'Cameo' is a thornless cultivar with double, peach-pink blooms.

Flowering quince (*Chaenomeles speciosa*)

Flowering quince (*Chaenomeles* x *superba* 'Rowallane')

Flowering quince (*Chaenomeles speciosa*)

Recommended Pruning

Season After flowering

Recommended Forms Informal bush

Shaping There is no need to shape this shrub because its natural form is graceful.

Maintaining Each year, cut back the shoots that flowered to strong buds. After the plant is a few years old, thin out poorly positioned or crossing growth, and cut back about a third to a fifth of the oldest shoots to the ground. This stimulates the growth of replacement shoots.

Restoring Cut out only a third of the shoots at a time, starting with the oldest and those that are crowded. Thin out new growth the following year before once again cutting out a third of the growth. Do this the third year, as well, and the shrub will have been restored.

Clethra spp.

Sweet Pepper Bush, Summersweet
CLETHRACEAE

Sweet pepper bush adds both beauty and fragrance to the summer garden.

Hardiness Zones 5–9

Size 2 to 30 feet tall, 4 to 20 feet wide

Appearance Leaves are alternate, dark green, shiny, and can be finely to deeply toothed. They turn a striking orange-red color in autumn. Individual flowers are bell- or cup-shaped, small, and white to greenish to pink. They grow in racemes or panicles, often upright but sometimes pendant.

Exposure Partial or dappled shade

Soil and Water Grow in very moist, acidic, humus-rich, fertile soil that is well-drained.

Comments Sweet pepper bush is native to the Eastern U.S. and Canada and is a valuable addition to any planting. It spreads by stolons, not by seeds, but is easy to contain. There are about 60 species and many cultivars. *C. alnifolia* 'Pink Spires' has light pink blooms, while 'Hummingbird', a dwarf form that grows only 2 to 3 feet tall, has masses of pure white blooms that perfume the entire garden. Japanese Clethra (*C. barbinervis*) is a much larger plant, reaching 30 feet tall in good conditions, and is noted for its 4- to 6-inch-long racemes of white flowers.

Summersweet (*Clethra alnifolia*)

Summersweet (*Clethra alnifolia*)

Japanese clethra (*Clethra barbinervis*)

Recommended Pruning

Season Late winter or early spring

Recommended Forms Informal bush

Shaping Unnecessary because the natural form is graceful

Maintaining Cut old stems back to the ground, and thin the weakest suckers. Thin damaged and crossing or crowded growth.

Restoring Cut back about a third of the stems each year for three years. When new growth appears, thin out the weakest stems and leave the strongest.

Cotoneaster spp.

Cotoneaster
ROSACEAE

The more than 200 species of cotoneasters include both deciduous and evergreen shrubs, most of which have brilliant red, orange, or shiny white berries in the fall.

Hardiness Zones 6–8

Size Ranging from 1 to 15 feet tall and 6 to 10 feet wide

Appearance Cotoneaster leaves are oval, elliptical, or rounded; glossy and mid- to deep green; and grow alternately on the branches. Spring and early summer flowers are pink, red, or white and are followed by the berries that persist into winter.

Exposure Deciduous species thrive in full sun; most evergreen and semi-evergreen species do well in full sun to partial shade, although the dwarfs require full sun.

Soil and Water Grow in moderately fertile, well-drained soil. Most species tolerate occasional dry periods.

Comments Good cultivars include the Peking cotoneaster (*C. acutifolius*), which is hardy to Zone 4 and grows to 10 feet tall and wide. *C. adpressus* is a rock garden favorite because it grows only a foot high, and the deciduous leaves turn a brilliant red before dropping in autumn. Rockspray cotoneaster (*C. horizontalis*) is popular with gardeners because of its manageable 3- to 5-foot-tall height and habit that is naturally tiered.

Bearberry cotoneaster (*Cotoneaster dammeri* 'Skogholm')

Willowleaf cotoneaster (*Cotoneaster salicifolius*)

Recommended Pruning

Season Prune deciduous species in late winter or early spring. Prune only to thin out crowded or crossing branches. Evergreen species don't require much pruning either, but crowded or crossing growth can be removed after the plants fruit, in mid-to-late summer.

Recommended Forms Informal bush except for hedge cotoneaster (*C. lacteus*), which can be pruned as a formal bush, and the prostrate cultivars that are allowed to sprawl.

Shaping Most cotoneasters require very little pruning aside from thinning crowded or crossing growth. See page 40 for pruning directions for hedges.

Maintaining Examine the plants every year, and thin as necessary. If the plant is not dense enough, cut back several inches to just above a bud growing in the direction you want to fill.

Restoring Thin out all excess growth at once on deciduous plants. Thin over a period of two years in the case of evergreens.

Creeping cotoneaster
(*Cotoneaster adpressus*)

Rockspray cotoneaster
(*Cotoneaster horizontalis*)

Japanese cedar (*Cryptomeria japonica* 'Benjamin Franklin')

Cryptomeria japonica 'Globosa Nana'

Japanese Cedar
TAXODIACEAE

This Japanese cedar is a dwarf plant that is a garden favorite because it makes an excellent shrub for a mixed border or specimen plant.

Hardiness Zones 5–8

Size 2½ to 5 feet tall, 2½ to 3 feet wide

Appearance This compact shrub has a naturally mounded habit. Needles are clear green when the plant is young, become bluish green as it ages, and turn a rusty red in extremely cold weather. The needles, which grow in whorls, persist for 4 or 5 years before falling and being replaced.

Exposure Full sun, but plants will tolerate partial shade.

Soil and Water Plants thrive in fertile, moist, and light soils with a pH range of 6.0 to 6.7, but will tolerate heavy clays in good light conditions.

Comments Larger Japanese cedars are also available. If you have a spot where a pyramidal form would be suitable, look for *C. japonica* 'Benjamin Franklin', which really qualifies as a tree because it can grow as tall as 40 feet in good conditions.

Dwarf Japanese cedar (*Cryptomeria japonica* 'Globosa Nana')

Dwarf Japanese cedar (*Cryptomeria japonica* 'Globosa Nana')

Recommended Pruning

Season This plant rarely needs pruning, but if a branch is damaged, cut it out when you first notice it.

Recommended Forms Informal bush

Shaping Allow the plant to grow naturally.

Maintaining Examine the plant every spring to check for winter-damaged growth, and thin it out if necessary.

Restoring Remove dead or damaged growth, and trim back branch tips in late winter to early spring.

Dwarf Japanese cedar (*Cryptomeria japonica* 'Globosa Nana')

Daphne spp.

Daphne
THYMELAEACEAE

The fragrance of blooming daphnes is reason enough to grow these plants, but their good looks and compact habits also endear them to most gardeners.

Hardiness Zones Depending on species, 4–8

Size 3 to 4 feet tall, 2 to 4 feet wide

Appearance Plants are naturally mounded. Clusters of white or pink, tubular flowers open on branch tips in spring. The glossy leaves are oval to elliptical and may be variegated in cultivars such as *D. odora* 'Aureomarginata'.

Exposure Full sun

Soil and Water Well-drained, moderately fertile soil with consistently moist moisture levels

Comments Favorite cultivars include the rose daphne (*D. cneorum*), which grows only a foot tall and makes a good edging or rock garden plant. *D.* x *burkwoodii* 'Carol Mackie' is a variegated form that has lovely pink flowers. The most hardy cultivar is *D.* x *burkwoodii,* which survives in Zone 4 winters.

Daphne (*Daphne* x *burkwoodii* 'Carol Mackie')

Rose daphne (*Daphne cneorum*)

Daphne (*Daphne* x *burkwoodii* 'Somerset') in late spring

Variegated winter daphne (*Daphne odora* 'Aureomarginata')

Recommended Pruning

Season After blooming is finished

Recommended Forms Informal bush

Shaping These shrubs are naturally well-formed and require no shaping.

Maintaining Examine the plant every year, and remove any dead or crossing branches after flowers fade. Trim branch tips to increase density at the same time.

Restoring Thin out crowded or crossing growth while the plant is dormant. Cut back long branches after blooming.

Fothergilla spp.

Fothergilla, witch alder
HAMAMELIDACEAE

In the same family as witch hazel, these plants are also early spring bloomers that add both fragrance and beauty to the garden.

Hardiness Zones 5–8

Size 2 to 10 feet tall and 2 to 5 feet wide

Appearance Shrubs are light and airy and, when in bloom, have an ethereal appearance. Leaves are leathery and oval, with obvious veination. The visible parts of the bottlebrush-like white or cream colored flower spikes are actually stamens. Leaves turn brilliant orange, red, and yellow in autumn before dropping.

Exposure Full sun

Soil and Water Plant in well-drained, high-humus soil with moderate fertility levels and a pH below 6.0. Plants require sustained moisture levels.

Comments Among favorite species is the dwarf, *F. gardenia,* and its many cultivars, including 'Jane Platt', known for its brilliant fall color. Large fothergilla, *F. major,* grows to 10 feet tall and is reliably hardy in Zone 5.

Large fothergilla (*Fothergilla major*) in spring

Dwarf witch alder (*Fothergilla gardenii*) in fall

Dwarf witch alder (*Fothergilla gardenii* 'Mount Airy')

Recommended Pruning

Season Late winter or early spring

Recommended Forms Informal bush

Shaping This plant requires very little pruning. If you want to make the growth a bit more dense, cut back branch tips after the plant blooms.

Maintaining Thin out old or poorly positioned branches in late winter.

Restoring If the shrub is severely overgrown, thin out poorly positioned branches entirely in late winter, and cut back the branches you'll retain to about 12 to 18 inches above the soil surface. The following year, thin the new growth if it is crowded or crossing.

2 *Pruning Perennials & Shrubs*

Daphne, Fothergilla

Hydrangea spp.

Hydrangea
HYDRANGEACEAE

Cheerful hydrangeas add beauty to any spot where they grow—in an informal hedge, as specimen plants, or even in mixed borders.

Hardiness Zones 3–9

Size 6 to 8 feet tall, 3 to 5 feet wide

Appearance Naturally mounded, hydrangeas have large, dark green leaves that are oval and heavily veined in most species. Blooms are ivory or, depending on the pH of the soil, pink or blue. In acid soils with a pH of 5.0 to 5.5, flowers of many species are blue, and in alkaline soils of 6.0 to 6.5 or higher, they are pink. In most species, clusters of flowers open to form a dome, but Lacecap hydrangeas (*H. macrophylla*) are composed of many tight buds surrounded by open flowers only on the perimeter of the dome.

Exposure Full sun

Soil and Water Plants thrive in well-drained soil of moderate fertility that is consistently moist, but will tolerate the occasional dry period.

Comments Favorite cultivars include the oakleaf hydrangea (*H. quercifolia*) with its leaves that truly are shaped like oak leaves and long cones of white flowers that turn to rose as they age. Snow hydrangeas (*H. arborescens* 'Grandiflora') are a mainstay of cold climate gardens because they are reliably hardy to Zone 3.

Peegee hydrangea (*Hydrangea paniculata* 'Grandiflora')

Oakleaf hydrangea
(*Hydrangea quercifolia* 'Snow Queen')

Bigleaf hydrangea
(*Hydrangea macrophylla* 'All Summer Beauty')

Lacecap hydrangea (*Hydrangea macrophylla* 'Blue Wave')

Recommended Pruning

Season Late winter or early spring

Recommended Forms Informal bush

Shaping Hydrangeas need very little pruning.

Maintaining Leave old flower heads over winter because they give some protection to the buds for the following year. In early spring, cut back the old flowered stems to fat flower buds. Also thin old branches, and cut out any that threaten to make the shrub crowded.

Restoring Neglected hydrangeas respond well to being cut to within 12 to 18 inches of the soil surface. The following year, thin out any crowded growth, and from then on, prune as usual.

Kolkwitzia amabilis

Beauty Bush
CAPRIFOLIACEAE

Branches of the beauty bush are festooned with lovely pink blooms in late spring to early summer.

Hardiness Zones 5–9

Size 10 feet tall, 12 feet wide

Appearance This shrub is unremarkable when not in bloom. But in late spring, when the bell-shaped, pink flowers open, true to its name, it's a beauty. Leaves are dark green and oval, about 3 inches long, on long, arching branches. Leaves turn yellow before dropping in fall.

Exposure Full sun, will tolerate partial shade in hot climates

Soil and Water Plant in well-drained soil with high fertility and keep moderately moist throughout the year.

Comments Although there is only one species of the plant, breeders are now working on cultivars and have released 'Pink Cloud'. This cultivar was chosen for the deeper color of its blooms.

Beauty bush
(*Kolkwitzia amabilis*)

Beauty bush (*Kolkwitzia amabilis* 'Pink Cloud')

Beauty bush (*Kolkwitzia amabilis*)

Recommended Pruning

Season After flowering

Recommended Forms Informal bush

Shaping Cut back to outward facing buds on young growth each year.

Maintaining Cut back branches that flowered to strong buds after flowering. Cut out a third to a fifth of the old growth each year; this plant suckers, so you will always have a fresh supply of branches.

Restoring Cut back the entire plant to a sturdy framework about 1½ inches above the soil surface in late winter. The following year, thin the new growth. In subsequent years, carry out maintenance pruning as described above.

Philadelphus spp.

Mock Orange
SAXIFRAGACEAE

The fragrance alone is reason enough to grow a mock orange, and the beauty of the blooms, habit, and leaves adds to the pleasure you'll get from this shrub.

Hardiness Zones 4–8

Size 4 to 12 feet tall, 4 to 12 feet wide

Appearance Most *Philadelphus* species are deciduous with oval leaves that grow opposite each other and turn yellow before dropping in autumn. The white flowers tend to have prominent white or yellow stamens and may be single and cup-shaped or double with an almost ruffled appearance. Their fragrance is reminiscent of orange blossoms.

Exposure Full sun, but most species will tolerate partial shade in hot climates.

Soil and Water Plant in well-drained soil with moderate fertility. Keep moderately moist during the growing season, but allow the soil to become somewhat dry in winter, when the plant is dormant.

Comments Mock oranges bloom in late spring to early summer, depending on the climate where they grow. Favorite cultivars include *P.* x *irginalis* 'Natchez', which grows to 12 feet high and has semidouble to double blooms that repeat in midsummer. 'Minnesota Snowflake' has double flowers, is only 6 feet tall, and distinguishes itself by being hardy to Zone 4. Most other species are hardy only to Zone 5. The most fragrant cultivars include *P.* x *lemoinei* 'Innocence' and 'Avalanche'.

Mock orange (*Philadelphus* 'Buckley's Quill')

Mock orange
(*Philadelphus* x *lemoinei*)

Mock orange
(*Philadelphus* x *virginalis* 'Natchez')

Recommended Pruning

Season After blooming

Recommended Forms Informal bush

Shaping Mock oranges require very little shaping.

Maintaining After flowering, prune out about a fifth of the old branches each year, and cut back older branches to new shoots.

Restoring Give three years to the project of restoring a mock orange. In the first year, cut out all dead or damaged growth in the shrub, and cut back about one-third of the branches to 12 to 18 inches above the soil surface. The following year, thin out the excess branches that were stimulated to grow by pruning, and also cut back the next third of old growth. Repeat this in the following year. From then on, maintain as advised above.

Viburnum spp.

Viburnum
CAPRILOLIACEAE

The 150 species of viburnum are well-loved for their striking good looks, as well as for the fragrance of their flowers.

Hardiness Zones 4–8

Size 5 to 15 feet tall, 3 to 10 feet wide

Appearance Some viburnums are evergreen or semi-evergreen, but most of these naturally mounded shrubs have deep green leaves that turn brilliant orange, red, or yellow before dropping in autumn. The spring-bloom flowers form in clusters at branch tips. The pink, white, or pink-blushed blooms may be domed, ball-shaped, flattened, pendulous, or similar to lacecap hydrangeas in that a few flowers on the edges of the cluster open but most remain closed in tight little buds. Red, yellow, blue, or black berries follow the flowers and persist through fall and into the winter.

Exposure Full sun

Soil and Water Plant in well-drained, moderately fertile soil with moderate moisture levels. Plants can tolerate brief periods of drought.

Comments Favorite garden cultivars include V. x *burkwoodii* 'Mohawk', which is 8 to 10 feet tall that is hardy in Zones 4–8. Its white, snowball-shaped flowers have yellow centers and a strong fragrance reminiscent of cloves. *V. x carlcephalum* 'Cayuga' is reliably hardy only to Zone 6 and its flowers have a similar appearance to 'Mohawk's' blooms, but the berries are black. *V. plicatum* var. *tomentosa* 'Shasta' is a double-file viburnum, meaning that it forms horizontal branches and its white flowers are shaped like those of lacecap hydrangeas.

Double-file viburnum (*Viburnum plicatum variety tomentosa* 'Shasta')

Virburnum (*Virburnum x carlcephalum* 'Cayuga')

Viburnum (*Virburnum x burkwoodii*)

Viburnum (*Virburnum x burkwoodii*)

Recommended Pruning

Season After blooms have faded

Recommended Forms Informal bush

Shaping Viburnums require very little pruning aside from cutting out old or damaged wood. If a viburnum threatens to grow too tall, cut back the branch tips to outward-facing buds.

Maintaining Examine the plants during winter, and cut out any dead growth or poorly positioned branches. Cut back branch tips after the plant has bloomed in spring if you want to shorten the plant.

Restoring After examining the plant, cut out old or dead branches. On severely overgrown shrubs, cut back a third of the branches each year to 12 to 18 inches from the soil surface. Start with those in the center of the plant to open it up to light and air. The following year, cut out the extra shoots that your previous pruning stimulated, and cut back the next third of the old growth. Repeat the process in the third year. From then on, practice maintenance pruning.

chapter 3

pruning roses

Pruning Roses

Roses require pruning in order to remain healthy and productive. Unlike most perennials and many shrubs and trees, when left to themselves, roses become so overgrown that they become extremely susceptible to diseases, such as black spot, botrytis, and both powdery and downy mildew, as well as to the many caterpillars that thrive in humid environments.

However, unlike what you may have been led to believe, pruning roses is not actually difficult. There is no absolutely correct or incorrect way to do it, and there are sensible guidelines that you can follow to get outstanding results.

First of all, it's helpful to understand a rose's reaction to pruning. If you prune very heavily, the rose is likely to put out fewer flowers, because you will have pruned off most of the wood on which they form, but the ones that do grow will be large. If you prune lightly, the plant will produce more blooms, and they will be slightly smaller.

Sensible Guidelines

Time your pruning operations according to the type of rose you are growing. If you have planted a rose that grows on its own roots, as *R. rugosa* plants usually do, wait two or three years after planting to prune it. In contrast, wait only a year to prune a grafted rose.

Begin your pruning in spring by entirely removing any dead canes and dead stubs on live canes. Then clean out any weak or spindly growth and any crowded canes.

When you prune or trim a live cane or stem, make cuts at a 45-degree angle about ¼ inch above a dormant or sprouting bud, even when you are removing spent flowers or dead-heading.

Whenever possible, cut above a strong, outward-facing bud so that new shoots will grow in a direction away from the center of the plant. But feel free to select a bud that will force the new growth in the direction that suits you (and will result in a shapelier plant).

Prune canes by cutting about ¼ in. above an outward-facing bud. Angle the cut parallel with the bud or at a 45-deg. angle. This allows rainwater to run off the cut surface rather than pooling and creating an incubator for fungal diseases.

Creating standard, or tree, roses requires careful selection of the rootstock and top growth, as well as rigorous pruning while the stem, or "trunk," is being established and throughout the life of the plant.

As a general rule, move down the cane and make your cut just above a leaf with five leaflets. However, some rose cultivars only have three leaflets per leaf, and others have seven, nine, or more. So when necessary, make your cut just above a healthy leaf at any place that suits you, whatever the number of leaflets.

You can deadhead a rose simply by pinching the old flower off at its base. Experiments have shown that it won't mind a bit and will go on putting out new growth and flowers just as if you had followed the rules and cut it above a leaf with five leaflets.

Pruning Time

A gardener's old saw says to prune all bush or shrub roses before the buds begin to break in early spring, but to wait to prune climbing roses until after they have bloomed.

This wasn't a bad rule in earlier times. Back then, most of the popular garden roses were repeat-flowering and bloomed on new wood that grew during the same flowering season. In contrast, most climbing roses of that time bloomed only once, early in the year, on old wood that had grown during the previous season. Because of this, when climbing roses were pruned early, too much of the flowering wood was removed.

Contemporary pruning times. Today, most climbing roses are repeat-flowering and bloom on new wood or on both old and new wood. Prune these plants in late winter or early spring, as you do other repeat-flowering roses. Also, some once-flowering bush and shrub roses bloom on old wood and shouldn't be pruned until after they've finished flowering. Therefore, it's more appropriate to base your pruning schedule

When to Prune Roses

Prune repeat-flowering roses, including the climbers, while they are dormant. In spring, trim them, and tie the canes to horizontal supports.

Prune all roses in spring by removing dead, damaged, diseased, and weak canes and those that cross the center of the bush.

on whether your roses bloom repeatedly during the season or only one time, early in the year—that is, whether they bloom on new wood generated this year or old wood that matured the previous year.

In regions where roses don't experience the cold temperatures and winds of winter—but only in those regions—you can trim them as much as necessary any time after they've gone dormant and have hardened off. But this trimming isn't a substitute for the more formal pruning that you'll do later in the spring. (See "When to Prune Roses," opposite and below.) If you are unsure, contact your county extension service.

Hybrid tea roses are pruned quite severely in late winter each year.

Once-flowering roses bloom on "old wood"—the canes that grew the previous season. Prune them just after they bloom to give the plants time to grow.

Repeat-flowering roses. Formally prune all your repeat-flowering varieties—whether they are modern or antique, bush, or climbing—in late winter or early spring. Local rose societies often announce when the proper time has arrived, but you can also gauge it as Cynthia Dreibak wrote in 1927:

> *When the forsythia are dressed*
> *in golden posies,*
> *Get out those secateurs and prune*
> *your roses.*

After that first major pruning, deadhead repeat-flowering roses, and trim them lightly throughout the flowering season, up until about six weeks before the expected date of the first hard freeze.

Once-flowering roses. Prune all your once-flowering roses—most species roses, ramblers, and old European garden roses, as well as some climbing roses, both old and modern—in late spring or early summer, as soon as possible after they've finished flowering. This gives them a long season to develop wood that will bloom the next year. During the late winter pruning, they can be

'Rosa Mundi' (*Rosa gallica versicolor*) is pruned after it blooms.

trained and cleaned up with a light trimming. Because most of these roses will flower on wood that grew the previous summer, retain as much of it as possible.

Pruning by Type and Habit

Though roses are officially divided into two general categories: Modern Roses and Old Garden Roses, pruning methods differ depending upon the plant's inclusion in one of the groups that rosarians casually and informally refer to as "antique roses" or "modern roses."

The term "antique rose" has become a very general and all-embracing name for almost any type of rose not typical of the form and habit of the hybrid teas, floribundas, and grandifloras that became so popular during the last half of the twentieth century. They may be once-flowering species

'Sweet Inspiration', a floribunda rose, is pruned in late winter.

roses or old European garden roses, such as albas, centifolias, damasks, gallicas, and moss roses. They may be early repeat-flowering roses, such as chinas, bourbons, noisettes, tea roses, and hybrid perpetuals. Or they may be the even more recently developed, repeat-flowering types known generally as shrub roses, including types such as hybrid rugosas, hybrid musks, David Austin English roses, Buck roses, Meidiland roses, Romantica roses, Explorer roses, Pavement roses, and Simplicity hedge roses.

Pruning style. As a general rule, it's best to prune the oldest rose types and the cultivars closest to the original rose species the most lightly, and those with a habit and form most like the modern hybrid teas, floribundas, and grandifloras the most severely. But this doesn't have to be a hard-and-fast rule. Experiments by the Royal National Rose Society of England have demonstrated that when most roses are pruned and shaped with hedge shears, just like all the other landscape shrubs, they do just fine.

Rosa rugosa var. *alba* forms edible hips in fall. Prune in late fall or when the plant is dormant.

'Peace', a hybrid tea, is pruned in late winter.

Pruning hybrid teas and grandifloras. Plants in both of these classes are repeat-flowering and leggy with long flower stems. Prune them in late winter. Remove old, spent canes, and trim the remaining growth by one-third. For larger but fewer flowers, cut out all but four or five of the youngest, strongest canes, and shorten these by at least one-half to two-thirds. Trim any remaining lateral shoots back to one or two growth buds. For display or competition and to improve the size and quality of hybrid tea flowers, remove any side flower buds as soon as they begin to develop during the blooming season.

Pruning floribundas. Floribundas are repeat-flow-

ering roses. They vary in form and habit from leggy bushes to shrub types, but all of them have short-stemmed flower clusters. Prune the leggy varieties in late winter as you do hybrid teas; prune the shrub types less severely, much as you prune modern shrub roses.

Pruning species and wild roses. These roses tend to be once-flowering even though they have a variety of growth habits. Cut out the old, nonproductive wood, and trim the remaining canes by one-third to one-half or more after they flower. Remove untidy canes and deadwood in late winter, and lightly trim long canes at that time.

Pruning gallicas. These roses are spring-flowering and have a low, dense habit. Prune after they flower. Once the bush reaches a mature size, thin out the crowded canes, and trim the lateral shoots by one-fourth.

'**Madame Hardy**', a damask rose, is pruned after flowering.

Pruning albas, centifolias, damasks, and mosses. These once-flowering plants all have tall, lax growing habits. Shorten the canes and lateral shoots by one-fourth to one-third, and thin out the older, non-productive wood after the plants flower.

Pruning bourbons, portlands, boursalts, and autumn damasks. These roses usually have some repeat blooms—especially in the fall—on their long, flexible canes. Prune them in late winter by trimming the longer canes by about one-fourth to one-third, shortening the lateral shoots by one-half, and lightly pruning the tips of the remaining canes. Then lightly trim again after the first blush of flowers has finished.

Prune the four or five varieties of smaller, shrub-type bourbons and portlands in late winter as you do tea roses.

Pruning tea roses. These plants are repeat or almost continuously flowering, and they resemble modern shrub roses. Thin out the old and crowded wood, and shorten the remaining canes by no more than one-third because they tend to resent heavy pruning. Deadhead and lightly trim the plants for shape during the growing season.

Pruning noisettes. Noisettes are repeat-flowering pillar roses and climbers. Remove up to one-third of the older canes in late winter. Shorten the remaining canes by one-third and the lateral shoots to two or three buds. Continue to deadhead and to trim for size and form throughout the growing season.

Pruning hybrid perpetuals. Most hybrid perpetuals are repeat-flowering with willowy, upright canes and some lateral shoots. Prune them as you do modern hybrid teas by removing old, unproductive wood and shortening the canes by up to one-half. Trim the lateral shoots back to two or three buds; then continue to trim severely throughout the season to maximize the flower quantity.

Pruning chinas and hybrid chinas. These perpetual flowering roses have

'**Graham Thomas**', a modern shrub rose, is pruned in late winter each year.

'Bonica', a shrub rose, is pruned in late winter each year.

'Sally Holmes', a shrub rose, is pruned in late winter.

'Golden Showers', a large flowered climber, is pruned in late winter each year.

a twiggy, branching habit. Shorten the canes and lateral shoots by about one-third, and thin out crowded and worn-out wood on mature plants. Otherwise, just trim and shape these roses as you do any hedge plant.

Pruning modern shrub roses. These recurrent flowering plants have various forms and habits. When they're two or three years old, begin removing crowded and untidy canes and shortening the remainder by one-third each year. Otherwise, trim for shape and size.

Pruning hybrid rugosas. These plants are repeat-flowering and have a dense, arching habit. The blossoms are followed by colorful hips (fruit). In late winter, thin out the older wood and shorten the remaining canes by up to one-third. The hips mature only if the plants aren't dead-headed. Fortunately, not deadheading doesn't seem to reduce flowering of most rugosa varieties.

Pruning once-flowering ramblers and climbers. Plants in these categories can be quite vigorous and spreading. Remove about one-fourth of the older wood after the plants flower. Prune the remaining canes as severely as necessary for size and form, and trim the remaining lateral shoots back to two or three buds.

Pruning repeat-flowering ramblers and large-flowered climbers. Deadhead these plants to encourage reflowering. In late winter, remove about one-fourth of the older wood, and trim the remaining canes for size and form. Trim the lateral shoots back to two or three buds. Otherwise, cut the plant back to the size necessary to keep it in bounds.

pruning hedges

Pruning Hedges

Most trees and shrubs need very little pruning once they are established. But a hedge is a different story. Formal hedges need regular pruning to maintain their consistent shape and dimensions, and even informal hedges need some pruning now and then to keep them in bounds and to stimulate flowering and dense foliage. The most important rule for pruning a hedge—especially a formal one—is that the top of the hedge must be narrower than the bottom. Stop pruning at least six weeks before you expect the first fall frost, giving tender new shoots time to harden before the onset of cold weather.

New Hedges

For a full, bushy hedge, it is important that plants produce branches close to the ground as well as higher up. So you may need to do some judicious pruning shortly after planting. Yet, as stated often throughout this book, new plants establish healthy root systems quicker if a full head of leaves can create photosynthesis that feeds roots, and if end buds are allowed to create hormones that also stimulate root growth. With new plants, bear this in mind.

If you need to prune deciduous plants during their first year, head back the main stems as shown (top right). Do not head back conifers, however.

To guide the shape of a formal hedge as it grows, prune just to promote balanced growth. Prune deciduous plants moderately, and just trim the sides of conifers and broad-leaved evergreens. To even out the sizes of plants in a hedge, the rule is to prune strong growth lightly and weak growth hard. That's because harder pruning stimulates more vigorous growth; cut back strong growth by no more than one-third of its length and weaker growth by up to two-thirds as the hedge grows.

It's important to establish the desired shape when a hedge plant is still small, shearing it to a miniature of its intended full-grown shape. For a formal look, a flat top can serve well in regions with light snowfall.

Annual growth

Experts sometimes disagree on when to begin shaping a hedge. Because end buds produce hormones that help stimulate root growth, bare-root plants may get off to a better start if given a year to become established before pruning. Container and balled-and-burlapped plants tend to have better root systems that may allow pruning upon planting.

Pruned to shape

Eventual Appearance

Avoid This

Wedge and square shapes result in bare, leggy bottoms.

Consider These Options

Hedge cross-sectional shapes greatly affect where the lush, green growth occurs. Avoid wide or square tops that shield lower branches from needed sunlight. Make the base broader than the top by at least a few inches. In snow country, consider shapes that help deflect snow.

Inverted wedge and obelisk shapes result in lush growth, top to bottom.

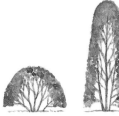

Rounded and pointed tops help deflect heavy snow loads.

Informally pruned, this hedge lets snow through.

Maintenance Pruning

The neat appearance of a clipped hedge can be maintained only by pruning twice a year with manual hedge shears or an electric or gas-powered trimmer. Follow guidance for specific plants given on pages 44–53.

Keep up with the maintenance of coniferous hedges. Because most conifers sprout new shoots only from new wood, only regular pruning of fresh new growth produces and maintains the fine, dense surface. Shear the light green new growth in spring before it hardens, two or three times at weekly intervals if necessary; shearing later in the season will leave unattractive wounds until the new season's growth begins.

Renewing an Old Hedge

Hedges that are regularly maintained can last for years. But if you've neglected your hedge or acquired a severely overgrown one, don't despair. Many deciduous hedges, as well as those of yew and of broad-leaved evergreens such as boxwood, can be saved. In general, those plants that respond well to hard pruning or renovation are likely to be the most successful candidates for hedge renewal.

One way to renew a hedge, especially an informal one, is to cut it down nearly to the ground and start over. A more complicated process, but one that retains some semblance of hedge throughout, is to cut back one side the first year and the other side the following year, as shown at right.

In either case, to promote strong growth, fertilize, mulch, and water the hedge well during the seasons before and after the renovation. Renovate deciduous hedges when they are dormant. But renovate evergreen hedges in midspring, as discussed on page 13.

Maintenance Pruning

With practice, many gardeners feel comfortable shearing hedges by eye, with either hand shears or a power trimmer. Most deciduous and evergreen plants with small, closely spaced leaves can be sheared. To maintain a neat formal hedge, you may need to shear at least twice a year, when new shoots have emerged but before their wood has hardened. To help control the power cable of an electric trimmer, drape it over your lead shoulder. Caution: make sure that your power cable meets manufacturer specifications for the trimmer and that it is protected by an outdoor-rated ground-fault circuit interrupter (GFCI).

Renewing an Old Hedge

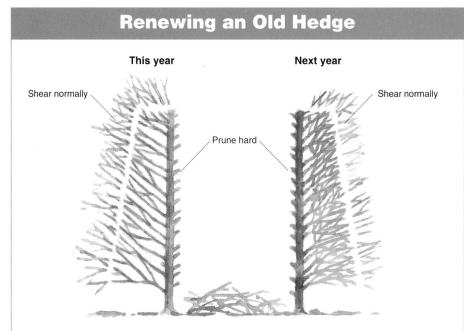

This year   Next year

Shear normally   Shear normally

Prune hard

To reduce the width of an overgrown hedge, prune back one side hard, as shown in the drawing at left, and then shear the other side as you would normally. During the next year, prune the other side hard, as shown at right, and shear the newly regrown side normally.

Southern yew (*Podocarpus macrophyllus*)

This tidy boxwood hedge and overgrown arbor create an arresting blend of formal and informal elements.

Southern yew (*Podocarpus macrophyllus*) is hardy only in frost-free climates and is pruned as yews (*Taxus* spp.) are.

Rose bay (*Nerium oleander*) make excellent informal hedges in frost-free climates and can also be pruned in late winter to make a formal hedge.

Berberis spp.

Barberry
BERBERIDACEAE

Barberries are loved for their colorful leaves and berries as well as the thorns on some species that discourage four-legged visitors to your yard.

Hardiness Zones 5–9

Size 1 to 12 feet tall, 1 to 12 feet wide

Appearance Both evergreen and deciduous barberries are commonly available and most are hardy in climates as far north as Zone 6. Leaves are oval and may be green, purple, reddish, or golden. Some, such as the Darwin barberry (*B. darwinii*) have spiked leaves, while in others, such as *B. mentorensis*, sharp thorns grow from the branches. Blooms form in clusters that hang from the branches, and red, purple, blue, and black berries follow.

Exposure Full sun to partial shade

Barberry (*Berberis thunbergii* var. *atropurpurea* 'Aurea')

Soil and Water Grow in well-drained, moderately fertile soil with moderate moisture levels.

Comments Evergreen barberries tend to have larger flowers than the deciduous species, but deciduous barberries are the most hardy and tolerant of harsh winter winds. Favorite cultivars include Wintergreen barberry (*B. julianae*), which is an evergreen that produces tremendous numbers of bright yellow flowers and blue-black berries. Its leaves have a single spike at the tip. The leaves of the semievergreen *B. x mentorensis* turn red in fall, while those of the deciduous cultivar 'Aurea' (*B. thundergii* var. *atropurpurea*) are golden until midsummer each year.

Darwin barberry (*Berberis darwinii*)

Recommended Pruning

Season After flowering

Recommended Forms Informal hedge, formal hedge

Shaping See page 41 for an illustration of pruning shapes. If you intend to prune the hedge into a formal shape, start shaping it only a year after first planting. To retain flowers, remember to wait until after the plant has bloomed to prune it.

Maintaining On evergreen species, remove damaged or dead branches every year, in midspring. Do this maintenance pruning when the plant is dormant on deciduous species.

Restoring See page 42 for an illustration of gradual renewal of a neglected hedge, using the appropriate timing for deciduous or evergreen species.

Dwarf Japanese barberry (*Berberis thunbergii* var. *atropurpurea* 'Crimson Pygmy')

Buxus

Boxwood
CUPRESSACEAE

These slow-growing evergreen shrubs with fine little leaves are the plants we think of when we imagine a formal hedge or fanciful topiary.

Hardiness Zones 5–8

Size 1 to 20 feet tall, 1 to 15 feet wide

Appearance Most boxwoods naturally grow into a neat, pyramidal form that makes a lovely informal hedge if only lightly pruned. The leaves are small and oval to lance-shaped. Somewhat inconspicuous male and female flowers grow on the same plant and bloom in spring.

Exposure Plants grow best in partial shade but will tolerate more sunlight in moist soils.

Soil and Water Plant in well-drained soils with good fertility. Keep moist throughout the year; plants do not do well in dry soils, particularly if exposed to bright light.

Comments Most species and cultivars have dark green, somewhat glossy or leathery leaves. However, the leaves of *B. sempervirens* 'Marginata' are variegated with a gold band around their perimeters, and *B. sempervirens* 'Elegantissima' has leaves with white margins. Small-leaved boxwood (*B. microphylla*) has leaves that turn bronze in winter.

Recommended Pruning

Season Late spring, after the main spurt of new growth

Shaping See page 41 for an illustration of pruning shapes. If you intend to prune the hedge into a formal shape, start shaping it only a year after first planting.

Maintaining Trim back the hedge in mid- to late spring, after it has flowered. Remove damaged wood at that time, too.

Restoring See page 42 for illustrated directions for restoring a hedge gradually. Box species can also tolerate being cut to the ground in late spring. Fertilize, water, and mulch well to promote strong regrowth.

English boxwood (*Buxus sempervirens*)

Littleleaf boxwood (*Buxus microphylla* 'Winter Gem') pyramidal trained

English boxwood (*Buxus sempervirens*)

X Cupressocyparis leylandii

Leyland Cypress
CUPRESSACEAE

This garden favorite makes an excellent evergreen hedge that not only screens out eyesores, but also serves to buffer roadside noises and prevent many animals from entering your yard.

Hardiness Zones 5–9

Size 60 to 70 feet tall, 8 to 15 feet wide

Appearance The foliage of most Leyland cypresses is a blue-green color, very fine, and overlapping like small green scales coating all the branches. It has inconspicuous blooms but rarely produces cones. The bark is a brownish red when the plant is young and gets gray when the plant is mature.

Leyland cypress (x *Cupressocyparis leylandii*)

Exposure Full sun

Soil and Water Plant in well-drained soils with moderate fertility and consistent, medium moisture levels.

Comments Leyland cypresses grow extremely quickly, putting on as much as 3 to 4 feet in height every season. Favorite cultivars include 'Naylor's Blue', which is hardy in Zone 5 and grows to an average height between 30 to 40 feet but can be 15 feet wide. If you are looking for a smaller cultivar, investigate 'Castlewellan', which is also hardy to Zone 5 and grows 20 feet tall and 5 feet wide. Its foliage also has a golden cast when young.

Leyland cypress (x *Cupressocyparis leylandii*)

Recommended Pruning

Season Midsummer, after the main spurt of new growth

Recommended Forms Informal or formal hedge

Shaping If shaping for a formal hedge, allow the tops to grow 6 to 12 inches taller than the intended height; then cut off the leaders to just above a lateral branch that is 6 inches below the intended height. It helps to set up posts with strings and use a level to make certain that you are cutting where you intend.

Maintaining Examine the plants every year, and cut out any dead or damaged growth. If you want regrowth to occur, do not cut into wood that lacks foliage.

Restoring Real restoration is very difficult to achieve. If the plant is simply too tall and bushy, cut back to below the intended height and width—as long as the wood there is still coated with healthy looking foliage. Otherwise, consider replacing the hedge with young plants that you can keep pruned.

Euonymus spp.

Euonymus, Spindle tree
CELASTRACEAE

Euonymus is prized for the gorgeous colors of it's foliage, as well as its berries.

Hardiness Zones 4–9

Size 20 feet high, 20 feet wide

Appearance This genus includes evergreen, semi-evergreen, and deciduous species and cultivars, some with brightly colored or variegated leaves. Flowers appear in groups of 3 to 15 in late spring or summer and develop into showy fruit that in some cultivars split open to show brightly colored seeds. Leaves are oval and growth is dense enough to make a good hedge.

Exposure Full sun for variegated and deciduous cultivars; evergreens can tolerate partial shade and are best protected from harsh winter winds.

Soil and Water Grow in well-drained soil with steady, moderate moisture levels. Deciduous species are tolerant of short periods when the soil is dry, particularly during winter.

Wintercreeper (*Euonymous fortunei* variety *radicans* 'Gracilis')

Comments The best cultivars for hedges include *E. alatus* 'Compactus', growing 6 to 10 feet tall. Leaves of this deciduous cultivar turn a brilliant red in autumn, and the fruits follow suit. This species is called "winged euonymus" because the stems taper into slender flanges. 'Rudy Haag' is an even smaller cultivar of the species, growing on 3 to 5 feet tall, making it ideal for low hedging. Plant this species only in built-up areas because birds spread the seed and it can take over wild areas.

Recommended Pruning

Season Late winter or early spring for deciduous species, and after flowering for evergreen species

Recommended Forms Informal bush

Shaping Euonymus require very little pruning. Trim back branches in early spring, but only if necessary.

Maintaining Examine the plants every year, and prune out dead or crossing branches when dormant, if the bush is deciduous, and in mid-spring if it is evergreen.

Restoring For deciduous species, see page 42 for illustrated directions for restoring a hedge. For evergreens, do not cut into old wood.

Winged euonymus (*Euonymus alatus*) winged twigs in winter

Dwarf winged euonymus (*Euonymus alatus* 'Compactus')

Ligustrum spp.

Privet
OLEACEAE

Privets are a favorite hedging plant because they are so versatile that they look good as informal hedges or when pruned into a rectangular, formal shape.

Hardiness Zones 3–10

Size 5 to 30 feet tall, 3 to 25 feet wide

Appearance This genus includes evergreen, semievergreen, and deciduous species, many of which make good hedges. The leaves can be oval or rounded and are usually glossy. Species such as *L. lucidum* 'Excelsum Superbum' have variegated leaves. Most species produce panicles of small, tubular, white or cream colored flowers that have a fragrance that some people dislike and others relish. Berries are black, blue, or purple and a favorite food for many birds.

Amur privet (*Ligustrum amurense*)

Exposure Full sun, especially for variegated cultivars. Green plants can tolerate partial shade.

Soil and Water Plant in well-drained soil with moderate fertility and moderate moisture levels.

Comments Flowers form in late spring and early summer.

A privet (*Ligustrum*)

Japanese privet (*Ligustrum japonicum*)

Recommended Pruning

Season After flowering

Recommended Forms Informal or formal hedge

Shaping After planting, cut back plants that will become a formal hedge to about a foot above the soil surface; then cut back the branches again later in the spring. This will encourage lots of branching. For the next two to three years, cut the plant back in early spring to encourage the base to fill out. After that, trim the plants after flowering to shape them.

Maintaining Each year, trim the plants after flowering to maintain their desired shape. Or if you do not want flowers, trim off the flower buds in spring. You may have to trim a formal hedge again in autumn to remove overly long growth. In winter, examine them and cut out any damaged wood.

Restoring See page 42 for illustrated directions on renovating a hedge.

Osmanthus spp.

Osmanthus
OLEACEAE

The dense growth, spiny leaves, and sweet fragrance that perfume the whole yard make many species of Osmanthus excellent hedges.

Hardiness Zones 6–9

Size 3.5 feet to 20 feet tall, 3.5 feet to 20 feet wide

Appearance The shrubs in this genus vary in appearance. Some, such as *O. x burkwoodii*, have oval, mid-green leaves with tiny teeth, while others, such as *O. heterophyllus* 'Purpureus', have deep teeth with spines and are a purple hue. *O. heterophyllus* 'Aureomarginatus' is also toothed and spiny but has yellow variegation on leaf margins. Blooms are tubular, white, and very fragrant. The berries that follow are blue-black.

Exposure Full sun to partial shade. Protect from winter winds and bright sunlight.

Soil and Water Grow in well-drained, fertile soil with moderate moisture levels during the growing season. Plants tolerate dry soils when dormant. *O. x burkwoodii* requires alkaline soils, but most thrive in neutral to acid soils.

Comments Hardiness varies among species. *O. fragrans*, which is the most strongly scented, is hardy only to protected spots in Zone 8. *O. x fortunei*, also hardy to Zone 8, blooms in fall, rather than spring as most of the sweet olives do. *O. heterophyllus*, Zones 7–9, also blooms in fall. *O. heterophyllus* 'Goshiki' grows only 3½ feet tall and wide and has leaves variegated with white that is often tinged pink-orange.

Recommended Pruning

Season After blooming for spring bloomers and in spring for fall bloomers

Recommended Forms Informal or formal hedge

Shaping Informal hedges require minimal pruning; cut them back to keep them in bounds. Formal hedges require heavy pruning when young to develop the desired shape. Prune according to bloom time, and head back overly long growth before midsummer.

Maintaining Thin out any dead or diseased growth in late spring. Trim to keep desired form once it is established.

Restoring See page 42 for illustrated directions.

Devilwood (*Osmanthus americanus*)

Chinese olive (*Osmanthus heterophyllus*)

Sweet olive (*Osmanthus fragrans*)

Sweet olive (*Osmanthus fragrans*)

Photinia spp.

Christmas Berry
ROSACEAE

Both evergreen and deciduous species are widely available, although the evergreens are the most frequently used for hedges.

Hardiness Zones 4–9

Size 6 to 40 feet tall, 6 to 25 feet wide

Appearance The most striking thing about most *Photinia* species is the red coloration of young evergreen leaves. Flowers are small and form in groups. The berries, for which the plant gets its common name, are generally red or orange-red.

Exposure Full sun or partial shade

Soil and Water Plant in well-drained soil with good fertility and medium to low moisture levels.

Comments These shrubs are members of the rose family and are susceptible to rose diseases, including black spot and fireblight, so they may not be the best choice for a hedge in humid climates where these diseases thrive. But if you can grow disease-free roses, take advantage of the year-round beauty of Christmas Berries. Evergreen *P. x fraseri* is a favorite hedge plant because of its lavish flower display and hundreds of bright red berries, as well as foliage that is a red or bronze color for weeks before becoming glossy green.

Japanese photinia (*Photinia glabra*)

Fraser's photinia (*Photinia x fraseri*)

Fraser's photinia
(*Photinia x fraseri* 'Red Robin')

Recommended Pruning

Season Late winter and early summer

Recommended Forms Informal or somewhat formal

Shaping For a hedge that you want to shape into a somewhat formal form, cut young plants back hard in late winter for the first several years to form the basic shape. In late summer, cut back branch tips to promote bushier growth. After that, selectively trim off overly long growth in summer.

Maintaining Thin out any dead or diseased growth in late winter or early spring. Trim plants to shape when the plant is dormant. Head back branch tips in summer to promote denser growth or trim back long branches.

Restoring See page 42 for illustrated directions.

Podocarpus spp.

Southern Yew
PODACARPACEAE

If you live too far south to grow yew (*Taxus* spp.), this plant makes an excellent substitute, partially because it is a distant relative.

Hardiness Zones 7–10

Size 6 to 70 feet tall, 6 to 30 feet wide

Appearance The needles of this evergreen, coniferous genus look like a softer version of yew needles: long and narrow. Plants bear male or female flowers, with red or blue berries forming only on the female plants. Female flowers are solitary, but male blooms form in catkins.

Exposure Full sun

Soil and Water Grow in well-drained soil with high humus and fertility levels. They thrive in high humidity areas. Protect from cold, drying winds.

Comments The easiest species to grow as hedges include the Tasmanian podocarp (*P. alpinus*), which is hardy to Zone 7 and grows only 7 feet tall. *P. novalis*, or Alpine totara, is similar in both hardiness and size but differs in appearance. Its needles are more rigid and have a slight bronze-colored tint. *P. macrophyllus*, which is sometimes known as Buddhist pine, is also hardy to Zone 7, but if left unpruned, can grow 50 feet tall and 25 feet wide. Fortunately, it is easy to prune into a manageable size. Also, in the cooler parts of its range, Zones 7 and 8, it tends not to grow beyond shrub size.

Southern yew (*Podocarpus macrophyllus*)

Southern yew (*Podocarpus macrophyllus*)

Southern yew (*Podocarpus macrophyllus*)

Recommended Pruning

Season Summer

Recommended Forms Informal or formal hedge

Shaping Informal hedges require very little pruning other than trimming to keep in bounds. To shape a formal hedge, immediately cut back plants to about a foot above the soil surface and then cut back the branches again later in the summer. This will encourage lots of branching. For the next two to three years, cut the plant back in summer to encourage the base to fill out. After that, trim the plants after flowering to shape them.

Maintaining Thin out dead growth in late winter or early summer. Cut back in summer to maintain shape.

Restoring See page 42 for illustrated directions.

Spirea spp.

Bridal-Wreath
ROSACEAE

This shrub becomes the focal point of the garden when its lovely, arching branches are lavishly coated with clusters of white or yellow blooms.

Hardiness Zones 4–9

Size 3 to 12 feet tall, 3 to 10 feet wide

Appearance This genus includes 80 species, some evergreen, but most deciduous. All bear showy clusters of small flowers in spring or summer, depending on species, and blooms can be white with white centers, white with yellow centers, pink, rose, purple, or even yellow. They can form in flattened domes or drooping panicles, depending on the species. Leaves of most are green, but some cultivars have yellow leaves.

Exposure Full sun

Soil and Water Grow in well-drained soil with good fertility and medium to high moisture levels.

Japanese spirea (*Spiraea japonica* 'Anthony Waterer')

Japanese spirea (*Spiraea japonica* 'Anthony Waterer')

Recommended Pruning

Season Prune plants that bloom on the current season's growth—the summer bloomers such as *S. japonica*—in spring. These can be cut back hard because they grow quickly. Prune spring-bloomers, which are the majority of *Spirea*, after flowering.

Recommended Forms Informal bush

Shaping There is no need to shape these plants; they form naturally pleasing bushes.

Maintaining Cut back summer bloomers hard in spring, and thin out all dead or poorly positioned branches. Thin out about a third of the old branches on spring blooming plants every year so the plant is continually replacing itself.

Restoring See page 42 for illustrated directions.

Comments There are hundreds of excellent cultivars, most of which make good informal hedges. *S. japonica* 'Goldflame' has red, copper, and orange leaves, making it a very showy hedging plant. 'Limemound' has bright yellow foliage with a russet tinge that takes on a lime-colored tint in summer. In fall, the leaves turn orange-red before dropping. *S. japonica* 'Anthony Waterer' has deep pink blooms and the foliage is sometimes variegated.

Japanese spirea (*Spiraea japonica* 'Goldflame')

Taxus spp.

Yew
TAXACEAE

Yews are versatile. They make attractive formal and informal hedges while also serving as excellent sources of bird food during the fall and winter.

Hardiness Zones 4–8

Size 3 to 30 feet tall, 3 to 16 feet wide

Appearance The slender, dark green needles of this evergreen conifer naturally look tidy and well-groomed. In most species, they are a dark green color. Flowers are inconspicuous, but the bright red berries, with their unusual bell-like shape, are bright red.

Exposure Full sun, partial shade, deep shade

Soil and Water Grow in well-drained, fertile soil. A few cultivars prefer a neutral to slightly acid soil but most tolerate more acid conditions. Check with your supplier about the pH requirement when you buy the plant.

Comments The variety you'll find in yews, in addition to their ability to tolerate some shade, means that unless you live in Zones 9 or warmer, you'll be able to find a yew for your purposes. For a manageable hedge, consider the English yew, *T. baccata* 'Adpressa Fowle', which grows to 6 feet tall and 16 feet wide. This plant requires a pH of 7 to 7.5 and is not suitable for soils that are naturally acid. 'Nana', a dwarf cultivar of Japanese yew (*T. cuspidate*), grows only 3 feet tall by 6 feet wide and is hardy in Zones 4 to 7. Hybrids between English and Japanese yews (*T. x media*) range is size from the 3-foot-tall 'Flemer' to the 12-foot columnar favorites 'Hicksii' and 'Hatfieldii'.

English yew (*Taxus baccata* 'Standishii')

Intermediate yew
(*Taxus x media* 'Hicksii')

Intermediate yew (*Taxus x media*)

Intermediate yew (*Taxus x media* 'Hicksii')

Recommended Pruning

Season Early spring for cutting back to size, and summer pruning for stray branches that are growing too long.

Recommended Forms Informal or formal hedge

Shaping Informal hedges require very little pruning other than trimming to keep in bounds. To shape a formal hedge, immediately cut back plants to about a foot above the soil surface when you plant and then cut back the branches again later in the summer. This will encourage lots of branching. For the next two to three years, cut the plant back in both spring and summer to encourage the base to fill out.

Maintaining Thin out any growth that looks dead or is in a poor position in early spring. Also trim to maintain the desired shape or increase density.

Restoring See page 42 for illustrated directions.

chapter 5

pruning trees

Pruning Trees

Pruning young trees is relatively straightforward. Unless you are pruning a fruit tree (discussed on pages 80–91), the primary reason to prune is to create a strong, well-balanced framework of branches. This not only results in a more attractive tree, it also results in one that is healthier and more resistant to damage from heavy snows or high winds. Once the framework has been developed, your other major pruning job with the trees in your yard is maintenance. You'll need to remove dead, damaged, or diseased growth when it occurs, and occasionally head back branches that threaten to interfere with such things as overhead power lines or buildings.

As your trees grow and you gain practice as a pruner, you are likely to begin enjoying the process. Nonetheless, it's still sensible to choose trees that won't require too much pruning once they are mature. When selecting trees, consider their natural growth habits, mature size and shape, and flowering and fruiting characteristics. For example, you would give yourself unnecessary work and aggravation if you planted a sugar maple (*Acer saccharum*), which typically grows to 75 feet tall, so close to a one story shed that you'd have to remove branches from one side of the tree as it grew.

People once believed that it was good for a tree to cut it back when you planted it. However, research has shown that the end buds on the branches send growth-promoting hormones to the roots. Young trees also benefit from the nourishment that leaves provide while the tree is getting established. So the current recommendation is to wait until the second year after planting to begin to shape it.

Plan your cuts well and do it gradually. If you remove too much wood at once, growth is slowed and the tree is weakened. Look at the tree to find its natural shape. No matter whether it is a conifer or deciduous tree, if it grows into a cone or pyramid shape, it has a single leader—or vertical trunk—with side branches that extend from it. In contrast, open-centered, or vase-shaped, trees are those in which the main trunk divides into several main branches. This form is generally given to small fruit trees, such as plums, and it is rare to see it in a landscape tree.

Pruning creates strong, healthy trees.

Same Container Plant: Different Results

This shows the hypothetical effects of three different pruning philosophies over several years.

Original container tree at planting

Thick, strong trunk

Moderately thick trunk

Slim, weak trunk

Option 1. Unpruned, this tree's energy has gone into side-branch and trunk growth, rather than height. At this stage, begin removing lower branches gradually over a period of years.

Option 2. Here, the lower side branches were pruned back about one-third at planting time, resulting in moderate growth. At this stage, begin removing lower branches from the bottom up.

Option 3. All lower side branches were pruned at planting time, so nearly all energy has gone into top growth, leaving a slim, weak trunk. Options 1 or 2 would have been better.

Most landscape trees have a length of bare trunk and a branched crown. Lower limbs are removed over the years to give more clearance under the tree, and in some cases, the central leader—or main trunk—is cut back at a certain point to create a bushier look. However, the tree will try to revert to its natural form and a new branch will try to take over as the main trunk, so this isn't recommended unless you are able and willing to spend a lot of time pruning back the tree every year.

Instead, leave the trunk alone, but as the tree grows, prune off branches that form narrow angles with the trunk and those that threaten to crowd the interior of the tree or don't conform to the shape you are fostering. Prune off all suckers growing from the roots and all watersprouts, or branches that grow upright from the limbs. Remove damaged or dead growth when you see it, and trim branch tips to shape the tree.

Pruning Deciduous Trees

The best time to prune most deciduous trees is late winter to very early spring, when the trees are dormant, meaning before the sap rises and the buds fill out before opening. There are some exceptions, though. Both birches and maples "bleed" heavily in spring, so it's best to prune them when they are fully dormant, in the dead of winter, or in late summer to early fall, when they lose less sap.

Same Tree: Different Results

Shaping

Inward-facing bud

Vertical structure

Spreading structure

Outward-facing bud

The above two illustrations show resultant growth if the same deciduous tree were pruned differently. In general, pruning cuts mainly above inward-facing buds will produce an inward and essentially vertical branching pattern, as shown at top. Pruning cuts mainly above outward-facing buds will encourage a spreading structure.

Encouraging Side Branching

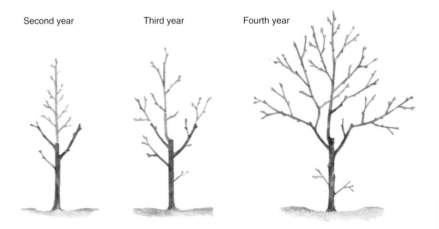

Second year   Third year   Fourth year

Promote more side branching of a tree with a strong central leader by removing the central leader in the second year and then removing leaders on all main branches in successive years to achieve the effects you want.

Creating an Open-Centered Tree

Second year   Third year   Fourth year

Create an open-centered tree by removing the central leader and encouraging growth that will result in the open-topped look.

Pruning can achieve practical and aesthetic purposes beyond general maintenance.

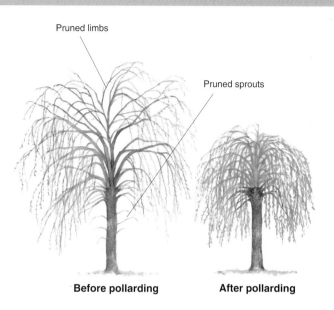

Pruned limbs

Pruned sprouts

Before pollarding   **After pollarding**

Pleaching. Branches of closely spaced trees can be interwoven to create a tall hedge supported by clean trunks; interweaving upper branches can create arches and tunnels. Though beautiful, pleached forms take a long time and a lot of work to achieve and are time-consuming to maintain.

Pollarding. Common in European landscapes, pollarded trees are severely cut back every year or so, often to the main trunk. This allows a tree to mature while retaining an artificially compact or even hedgelike form. Willows, beeches, and lindens are often given this severe treatment.

Espalier. The branches of an espaliered tree or shrub are trained flat against a vertical surface in an interesting, usually symmetrical, branching pattern. Espaliers save space, dress up a wall or fence, and provide variety in a small garden. Fruit trees take well to such pruning and bear larger fruit within reach for easy picking. Here are steps in training:

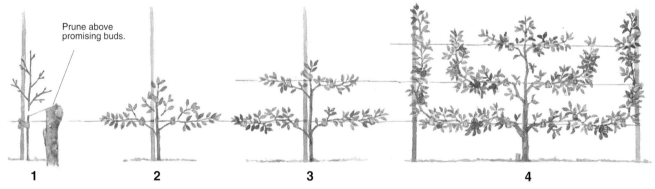

Prune above promising buds.

1   2   3   4

1. After your already-staked plant's roots are established, drive end posts at the distance you wish your espalier to spread. Then string a taut galvanized wire between the end posts, crossing the original stake a few inches above buds of desired shoots.

2. Prune all but the three best shoots. Tie the two horizontal shoots to the wire, and tie the vertical shoot to the stake. Use nonabrasive ties of biodegradable material.

3. When the vertical shoot reaches the desired height, string the second wire. Select the three best top shoots, and secure them as before. Continue securing and training first tier shoots outward, pruning any excess shoots.

4. After some years, the central trunk will support itself and its support stake can be removed. Continue pruning and training over the years.

A deciduous tree as it appears through the four seasons, clockwise from top left: spring, summer, fall, and winter.

You can prune all trees in summer to slow their growth and remove suckers and watersprouts. But try not to prune in fall unless you are repairing damage, because wounds heal more slowly then.

Pruning Conifers

Make your life easier by choosing conifers with a growth habit and mature size suitable for your location. Dwarf conifers are especially suitable for small properties. Although conifers seldom need regular pruning to achieve their natural shape, you can avoid struggling to keep growth in check if you choose carefully. Conifers described in this book are narrow-leaved (needled) and evergreen, except for the larch (*Larix*), which loses its leaves in fall.

All conifers have one of two distinct growth habits: random branching, with branches growing anywhere, and whorled branching, with multiple branches radiating from the trunk at spaced intervals. (See the illustrations at right.)

Most conifers need little more than removal of dead or damaged branches—or burned foliage—before growth begins. The best time to prune conifers to limit growth or improve shape is just after new growth appears. Some conifers accumulate unattractive, congested growth that should be removed to minimize damage from snow and ice.

Two Types of Conifers

Random-branching conifers

(Removed leader branches will usually be filled in by laterals.)
- Arborvitae
- Cedars
- Cypresses
- Hemlocks
- Junipers
- Yews

Whorled-branching conifers

(Removed leader branches aren't readily filled in.)
- Pines
- Firs
- Spruces

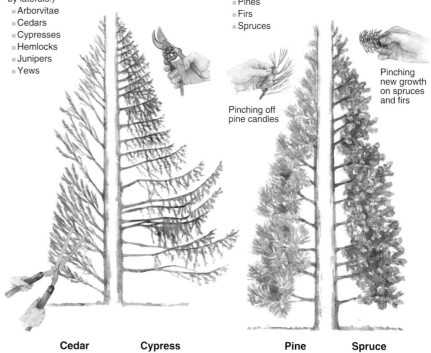

Pinching off pine candles

Pinching new growth on spruces and firs

Cedar   **Cypress**   **Pine**   **Spruce**

Branching Patterns. Conifer genera have one of two branching patterns: random branching, as shown at left, or whorled branching, as shown at right. Most random-branching conifers can be sheared and pruned to maintain size and to shape them into hedges and topiary art. Of the three whorled-branching conifers, pines don't respond well with new growth when pruned, but you can arrest growth by pinching back new-growth "candles" in spring. The other two whorled-branching conifers, the spruces and firs, can also be pinched back. Yet spruces and firs often have dense enough growth to allow some light shearing, mainly of new growth that won't be noticeable for long.

Leadership Training

Conifers achieve their characteristic central shaft of trunk because their top leader grows more strongly than other branches. If you want your tree to achieve that characteristic point, prune competing leaders, and replace a damaged leader by splinting it to a support as shown.

Prune the less desirable, competing leader.

Replace a broken or damaged leader by splinting the next most desirable branch.

Careless Pruning. Both photos show results of careless pruning. Above, careless lopping of this 1-in. apricot branch left a small protruding chunk of wood near the top of the cut, which prevents the collar from healing over it as quickly as it heals over surrounding edges. Above right, a single, top-to-bottom cut on the 4-in. branch of this arborvitae resulted in torn bark that exposes the tree to diseases and pests.

Clean Cuts. Proper pruning cuts just beyond the collar on this Kwanzan cherry resulted in the nicely healing wound shown at left and the almost completely healed wound on another branch, as shown above.

Rubbing Limbs. This pair of rubbing limbs will eventually abrade bark enough on one or both limbs to expose inner wood to disease and pests. One limb should be removed.

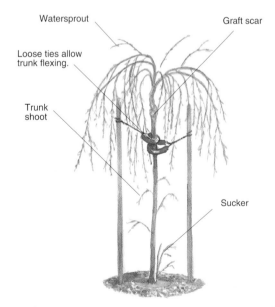

Watersprout

Loose ties allow trunk flexing.

Trunk shoot

Graft scar

Sucker

Spreading Shoots. Growers of fruit trees often spread young shoots to crotch angles greater than 45 deg., both to promote a strong connection at the collar and to keep limbs within reach for picking.

You can fashion spreaders from pruned branches, employing broad Y crotches at one end and inserting a galvanized nail, as shown, into the other, and then cutting its head off with side-cutting pliers.

Weeping Trees. Prune watersprouts on top-grafted weeping trees. Branches on natural, ungrafted weeping trees don't need pruning. They will eventually weep desirably. Prune dead branches, as well as lopsided or congested branches. Rub off soft shoots on the trunk with your thumb, and cut off other shoots and suckers.

Improper Pruning. The black ridge of bark on this paper birch shows why tight vertical crotches tend to be weaker than crotches with angles greater than 45 deg. Here, the bark of the trunk and branch have grown together, leaving this deep ridge, which has a weaker connection than shallower ridges that result when branches emerge at crotch angles greater than 45 deg. Correct pruning here would involve three cuts, as shown in the drawing

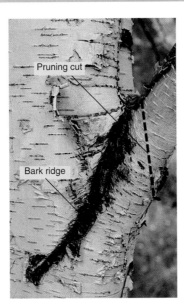

at right. The third cut would begin just outside the bark ridge at the top and proceed at roughly the angle shown by the dotted line in the photo.

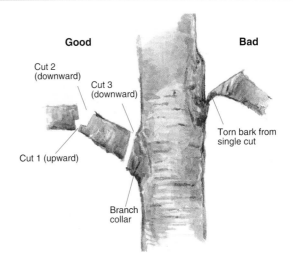

Large Limbs. To prune limbs of 1½ in. diameter or more, make a series of three cuts, starting about 1 ft. out from the collar. If you mistakenly make only one cut, above right, the branch will begin to fall before you're through, tearing bark away, retarding healing, and exposing wood to disease and pests.

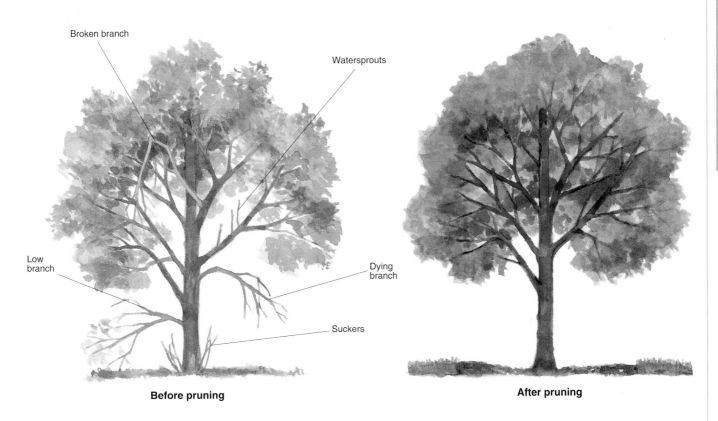

Perfect Pruning. These before and after drawings suggest how to prune an established deciduous tree for health and beauty. Always remove dead, broken, diseased, or crossing branches. Also remove watersprouts and suckers.

Abies spp.

Fir
PINACEAE

Native to mountainous areas in temperate and cold regions, firs look like a more graceful version of a spruce.

Fraser fir (*Abies fraseri*)

Hardiness Zones 3–8

Size 2 to 150 feet tall, 3 to 25 feet wide

Appearance Fir needles grow 2 to 3 inches long and are flat, usually with two white or silver bands on the underside. The female cones are 3 to 6 inches long and pale green when young, but develop a purplish cast as they mature. Male cones grow in the crown of the tree and are pendent. They mature from green to brown or purplish brown.

Exposure Full sun, but tolerate some shade

Soil and Water Grow in well-drained soil with good fertility and moderate moisture levels. They thrive in cool-summer regions. Plant where they are sheltered from harsh winter winds.

Comments When the needles are crushed, they produce a lemony scent. Of the many firs available, one of the best for the home landscape is the white fir (*A. concolor*). Although it is native to the Rocky Mountains, Zones 3–7, it adapts to Eastern and urban conditions, as well as heat and drought. Balsam fir (*A. balsamea*), Zones 3–5, is highly aromatic, and in more southern areas, Fraser fir (*A. fraseri*) is a good choice.

Recommended Pruning

Season After new growth begins

Recommended Forms Natural

Shaping Rarely necessary

Maintaining Examine trees in spring or after storms to check that they are not damaged. If damage has occurred, thin out the broken branch.

Restoring Not necessary

White fir (*Abies concolor*)

White fir (*Abies concolor* 'Glenmore')

Acer spp.

Maple
ACERACEAE

Maples are a favorite shade tree and are known for the brilliant colors of their leaves in autumn.

Hardiness Zones 4–9

Size 3 to 90 feet tall, 5 to 35 feet wide

Appearance Most maples have deeply lobed and toothed, mid- to deep green leaves, but species such as *A. carpinifolium* and *A. davidii* have unlobed leaves, and many of the Japanese maples (*A. japonicum*) have red leaves through the year. The seeds are winged and flutter to the ground when ripe.

Exposure Full sun to partial shade

Soil and Water Grow in well-drained soil with good fertility and moderate moisture levels.

Comments Whatever your landscape needs, one of the over 150 species and many hundreds of maples can probably supply it. For example, the Chinese paperbark maple (*A. griseum*), Zones 4–8, grows only 25 feet tall and has peeling, mottled bark. Its leaves turn red or bronze in fall. If you are looking for a large shade tree, investigate the sugar maples (*A. saccharum*), which grow to about 75 feet tall and give dense shade.

Sugar maple (*Acer saccharum*) in fall

Norway maple
(*Acer platanoides*) samaras

Chinese paperbark maple
(*Acer griseum*)

Recommended Pruning

Season Late autumn to midwinter

Recommended Forms Natural, single leader

Shaping Rarely necessary; head back overly long growth

Maintaining Examine trees in early winter to check for damaged or poorly positioned growth. Thin out crossing branches and those that are damaged.

Restoring Not necessary

Betula spp.

Birch
BETULACEAE

Birches, whether single-trunk or multistemmed, add a graceful note to any landscape but are particularly well suited to cool northern areas.

Hardiness Zones 2–9

Size 2 to 80 feet tall, 4 to 40 feet wide

Appearance Peeling white bark on slender stems marks most species of birch trees, although the bark of a few species is more pinkish brown than white, and on others, it doesn't peel. Both male and female catkins grow on the same tree, but the male catkins are the showy ones. They are 3 to 4 inches long, yellow-brown, and hang vertically. Leaves are small and pointed and sway easily in the wind. They turn yellow or golden before dropping in autumn.

Exposure Full sun or dappled shade

Soil and Water Grow in well-drained, moderately fertile, moist soil.

Comments Birches are fast growing plants but easily fall prey to the birch leaf miner if they are suffering from nutrient deficiencies and the bronze birch borer under various conditions. The river birch, *B. nigra* 'Heritage' (Zones 4–8), is largely resistant to pests and diseases and also tolerates both brief periods of flooding as well as dry soil in summer. It has buff pink rather than white bark, and the inner bark may be salmon pink to grayish, cinnamon, or reddish brown. Paper, or canoe, birch (*B. papyrifera*) has the whitest bark. Hardy in Zones 2–6, it is the birch that northern Native Americans used to sheathe their canoes. Both of these birches easily develop multiple stems, as described at right.

River birch (*Betula nigra*) catkins

River birch (*Betula nigra* 'Heritage')

Recommended Pruning

Season Late summer or fall; plants bleed excessive sap if pruned in early spring.

Recommended Forms Natural or multistemmed

Shaping To create trees with multiple stems, cut back the central leader above at least two or three buds in the second fall after planting. The following year, thin out poorly positioned stems and retain those growing away from each other. After the trunks are established, the plants require very little shaping.

Maintaining Examine plants to check for damaged growth, and thin it out during the summer and fall.

Restoring Unnecessary

Paper birch (*Betula papyrifera*) in fall

Carya spp.

Hickory, Pecan
JUGLANDACEAE

Hickory and pecan trees are beloved for their impressive size, ornamental bark, lovely fall colors, and often edible nuts.

Hardiness Zones 4–9

Size 80 to 100 feet tall, 50 to 70 feet wide

Appearance These tall trees generally have ridged or furrowed bark and opposite leaves with prominent veins. Leaves generally turn a vivid yellow in fall. Male and female flowers form on the same tree, and nuts are prolific.

Exposure Full sun or partial shade

Soil and Water Grow in well-drained, deep soil with moderate to high fertility and good humus levels.

Comments These magnificent trees are often grown as shade trees or specimen plants in large yards. Whether hickory or pecan, they produce hundreds of nuts, so are best positioned away from sidewalks and roads. Shagbark hickory (*C. ovata*), Zones 4–8, is often grown for its "shaggy" bark that forms in layers, as well as its lovely yellow fall foliage and huge crops of hickory nuts. Commercially, the tree is also grown for its aromatic wood, which can be used to smoke meats. Pecans (*C. illinoinensis*), Zones 5–9, are grown for their nuts, but also have ornamental bark and lovely yellow foliage.

Shagbark hickory (*Carya ovata*)

Pecan (*Carya illinoensis*) fruits (nuts)

Pecan (*Carya illinoensis*) in bloom

Shagbark hickory (*Carya ovata*)

Shagbark hickory (*Carya ovata*)

Recommended Pruning

Season Late winter or early spring

Recommended Forms Natural

Shaping Rarely necessary

Maintaining Examine the tree every year and remove any crossing or damaged branches.

Restoring Unnecessary

Cedrus spp.

Cedar
PINACEAE

Tall and graceful, cedars provide a focal point in the yard all through their long lives.

Hardiness Zones 5–9

Size 4 to 200 feet tall, 6 to 40 feet wide

Appearance Short needles grow in clusters on these lovely evergreen conifers. Species such as *C. deodara* are pyramidal in shape, while cedar of Lebanon (*C. libani*) matures into a tree with a flattened top. Male cones are about 3 inches long, and female cones are about 5 inches long.

Blue Atlas cedar (*Cedrus libani* subsp. *atlantica* 'Glauca')

Exposure Full sun

Soil and Water Grow in well-drained soil with moderate fertility. Cedar is tolerant of a wide range of soil conditions, including acidity and periods of drought.

Blue Atlas cedar
(*Cedrus libani* subsp. *atlantica* 'Glauca')

Comments Give cedars adequate space to grow to their full potential. Favorite cultivars include *C. libani* subsp. Atlantica 'Glauca', Zones 6–9. This 40- to 60-foot-tall tree has a flattened top and blue-green or silver-green needles. The species *C. libani*, known as cedar of Lebanon, is slightly more hardy and grows as tall as 120 feet. *C. deodara*, the deodar cedar, has beautiful, drooping branches and is hardy in protected spots in Zones 8–9. This pyramidal tree reaches 200 feet tall and 150 feet wide—don't plant it unless you have the space.

Deodar cedar
(*Cedrus deodara*)

Recommended Pruning

Season Late winter or early spring

Recommended Forms Natural form

Shaping Shaping is unnecessary unless two central leaders form. In that case, remove the weaker of the two and let the strong one develop.

Maintaining Examine the tree for signs of damage every winter or very early spring, and prune out all damaged wood.

Restoring Unnecessary

Cercis canadensis

Redbud
FABACEAE

Most cultivars have lovely red-purple or magenta buds that become apparent in early spring and open to rose-pink flowers at just about the same time the dogwoods bloom.

Hardiness Zones 4–9

Size 15 to 30 feet tall, 12 to 30 feet wide

Appearance Leaves often have a reddish tint when they first appear in spring and are heart-shaped. They mature to dark green, although they glow lime green when the sun shines through them. In fall, they turn bright yellow or gold before dropping. The blooms are shaped like pea flowers and the seedpods look like flattened peapods.

Exposure Full sun or dappled shade

Soil and Water Plant in moist but well-drained, fertile soil. Plants tolerate somewhat acid conditions.

Comments Redbuds resent transplanting, so place where they are to grow when they are only a year or two old. Favorite cultivars include *C. canadensis* 'Forest Pansy', with leaves that retain a reddish hue all through the season. Other *C. canadensis* cultivars include 'Flame', which has double blooms; 'Silver Cloud', which has silvery white variegation on the leaves early in the season; and 'Alba', a white-flowered tree. Chinese redbud, *C. chinensis*, is hardy only to Zone 6, in contrast to the *C. canadensis* cultivars that are hardy to Zone 4. *C. chinensis* is a multi-stemmed tree that is naturally graceful.

A white form of **eastern redbud** (*Cercis canadensis* variety *alba*)

Eastern redbud (*Cercis canadensis* 'Forest Pansy')

Multistemmed Chinese redbud (*Cercis chinensis*)

Recommended Pruning

Season Late winter or early spring

Recommended Forms Natural

Shaping Rarely necessary

Maintaining Examine plants in winter, and thin out any damaged growth. Some people "pollard" 'Forest Pansy' to stimulate it to grow larger leaves. Pollarding is cutting back all of the stems to 2 to 3 buds on each one. Mulch well to retain moisture. The plant will regrow in spring and create larger leaves. Because plants bloom on old wood, when you pollard them, you lose the flowers.

Restoring Unnecessary

Cotinus spp.

Smoke Tree
ANACARDIACEAE

The billowing, pinkish gray panicles of "smoke" this tree produces make it an ideal specimen plant in the yard or focal point in the shrub border.

Hardiness Zones 4–9

Size 10 to 30 feet tall, 15 to 25 feet wide

Appearance The showy leaves are alternate, oval to rounded, and green or purple. In autumn, they turn vivid colors before dropping. The bark on older trees is corky and ornamental. The flowers themselves are small and inconspicuous but grow in the long panicles that give the tree its common name.

Exposure Full sun or partial shade

Soil and Water Plant in well-drained soil that is moderately fertile, neutral to slightly alkaline, and generally moist.

Comments This tree is native to limestone soils in the United States, as well as parts of Europe. As a matter of fact, European smoke tree, *C. coggygria*, Zones 5–9, is often used in informal hedges or shrub borders because it grows only 15 feet tall. Cultivars include 'Velvet Cloak', with purple leaves through the summer that turn reddish before dropping in autumn. American smoke tree (*C. obovatus*) is hardy in Zones 4–8 and can reach 30 feet tall, although it is a slow grower.

Recommended Pruning

Season Late winter to early spring

Recommended Forms Natural. Many smoke trees are naturally multistemmed. This characteristic will be apparent on trees in nursery cans.

Shaping Shaping is unnecessary unless you are trying to keep the tree small. In that case, cut back to outward facing buds in early spring. Smoke trees can be pollarded, too, if you cut them back to 2 or 3 buds in late winter. Because they grow on new wood, they will bloom in early summer.

Maintaining Examine trees for damage in winter, and remove any damaged branches or those that cross.

Restoring Unnecessary

European smoke tree (*Cotinus coggygria*)

American smoke tree (*Cotinus obovatus*) in fall

European smoke tree (*Cotinus coggygria*)

Crataegus spp.

Hawthorn
ROSACEAE

This relative of roses forms beautiful red fruit that birds love as much as they love rose hips, so a hawthorn tree in your yard does double-duty.

Hardiness Zones 4–9

Size 20 to 25 feet tall, 12 to 30 feet wide

Appearance Hawthorns are closely enough related to roses to resemble them in a few respects. The dark green, alternate leaves are toothed or lobed and have a glossy sheen. Flowers look like small, single roses and are white, red, or pink with prominent yellow centers. Many species have thorny stems, and the thorns can be 3 inches long and quite sharp.

Exposure Full sun or partial shade

Soil and Water Grow in well-drained soil of average fertility. Because they are prone to the same fungal infections that strike roses, place them where ambient breezes will blow over their leaves.

Comments If you live in a humid climate, choose disease-resistant cultivars. One of the best is *C. viridis* 'Winter King'. Hardy to Zones 5–7, it grows from 20 to 30 feet tall and about 20 feet wide. The silvery bark exfoliates as the tree matures. Blooms are white and the fruit is bright red and round. The Washington thorn (*C. phaenopyrum*) is hardy over a much broader area—from Zones 4–8. It bears huge numbers of white flowers that are followed by red berries that persist into winter. It is commonly used in the United States and Canada, in both urban and rural settings.

Washington thorn
(*Crataegus phaenopyrum*)

Green hawthorn
(*Crataegus viridis* 'Winter King') in early spring

Green hawthorn
(*Crataegus viridis* 'Winter King')

Recommended Pruning

Season Late winter or early spring for trees. After flowering for hawthorns used as hedges.

Recommended Forms Plants naturally form a vase shape, and many have multiple stems.

Shaping Shaping is not often necessary except if you are pruning it to be an informal hedge. In that case, cut back branch tips to outward facing buds to make the plant more dense. In humid areas, this can increase disease incidence, so pay attention to the plant's response. If disease occurs, thin out crowded growth.

Maintaining Examine the plant for damage each year, and cut it out in late winter. Other than that, there is no need to prune.

Restoring Unnecessary

Fraxinus spp.

Ash
OLEACEAE

Generations of gardeners have planted these large, deciduous trees for lawn and shade trees because of their stately good looks and brilliant autumn colors.

Hardiness Zones 3–9

Size 30 to 100 feet tall, 40 to 50 feet wide

Appearance Leaves are opposite and long and pointed. They turn brilliant colors in fall before dropping. Many species bear winged fruit that contain the seeds, but seedless species and cultivars are also available. A few ash species bear ornamental flowers in spring, although both the male and female flowers, which are carried on the same tree, are more often inconspicuous.

Exposure Full sun

Soil and Water Grow in fertile, well-drained but moist, neutral to alkaline soil.

Comments Ashes grow quickly, so if you are looking for a tree that can provide shade within a few years of being planted, consider an ash species. The green ash (*F. pennsylvanica*), hardy to Zones 3–9, is 50 to 60 feet tall at maturity. It tolerates a wide range of conditions. For home landscapes, choose a cultivar such as 'Marshall's Seedless', because it is both disease-resistant and seedless. White ashes (*F. Americana*) reach 80 to 100 feet tall and are hardy in Zones 6–9. Cultivars such as 'Autumn Purple' and 'Autumn Glory' have brilliant red-purple leaves in fall in the north and a paler red in the south. Flowering ash (*F. ornus*), Zones 6–9, has fragrant, showy flowers and deserves to be planted more frequently.

Green ash (*Fraxinus pennsylvanica*) in fall

White ash (*Fraxinus americana* 'Autumn Purple') in fall

Recommended Pruning

Season Late winter and early spring

Recommended Forms Natural

Shaping Unnecessary

Maintaining Examine the tree every winter, and thin out any damaged wood.

Restoring Unnecessary

Flowering ash (*Fraxinus ornus*)

Ilex spp.

Holly
AQUIFOLIACEAE

Hollies are loved for their brilliant red, orange, yellow or blue-black shiny berries and glossy leaves that range from being spiny to having smooth edges.

Hardiness Zones 3–9

Size 3 to 80 feet tall, 3 to 15 feet wide

Appearance Hollies may be evergreen or deciduous and are variable in appearance. Some cultivars, such as *I. aquifolium* 'Aureo-marginata', have yellow variegated leaves and some, such as *I. opaca*, have green leaves. Male and female flowers are borne on separate plants, and most species require fertilization for berries to form. Dwarf hollies can be as small as *I. cornuta* 'Rotunda', which is 3 feet tall, and English hollies (*I. aquifolium*) can reach 80 feet tall at maturity.

Exposure Full sun or partial shade; variegated forms require full sun for good coloration.

Soil and Water Grow in well-drained, moist, moderately fertile and humus-rich, slightly acid soil.

Comments Tree hollies tend to be hardy only to Zone 4, although smaller species tolerate Zone 3 conditions. The American holly (*I. opaca*) grows wild in the east from Zones 5–9 and forms a 40- to 50-foot pyramidal tree. There are over 1,000 varieties of this holly. 'Foster holly #2' (*I. x attenuata*) is a good holly for the south, from Zones 6–9, and grows about 25 feet tall.

Recommended Pruning

Season Late winter or early spring

Recommended Forms Natural or formal

Shaping Hollies need very little pruning if you are growing them in their natural form. If you are shaping them into a form such as a topiary, concentrate on this when they are young. Cut back branch tips in summer. If growing as a hedge, trim in late spring or early winter.

Maintaining Examine plants in winter, and thin out any damaged growth.

Restoring American holly is the only holly that does well when cut back severely. If you have an old tree that you'd like to restore, cut it to a foot or so above the soil surface in very early spring. The following year, thin out the excess growth that formed the first summer. After that, the tree will need very little pruning.

English holly (*Ilex aquifolium*)

American holly
(*Ilex opaca*)

Variegated English holly
(*Ilex aquifolium*
'Aureorginata'),

Laburnum spp.

Golden chain tree
LEGUMINOSAE

This small, deciduous tree is luminous in spring when chains of fragrant, bright yellow blooms drip from its branches.

Hardiness Zones 6–8

Size 20 to 30 feet tall and wide

Appearance Leaves are alternate and divided into three leaflets. The flowers are shaped like pea flowers and form in long racemes.

Exposure Full sun

Soil and Water Plant in well-drained soil that is moderately fertile.

Comments There are only three species of golden chain trees, *L. anagyroides*, which is often called common laburnum, and *L. alpinum*. A common hybrid form is *L. x watereri*, which is a cross between the two species. Both of the two most common cultivars are *L. x watereri* plants. 'Alford's Weeping' is known for its spreading crown, and 'Vossii' for the flower racemes that can be up to 24 inches long.

Waterer hybrid laburnum (*Laburnum* x *watereri* 'Vossii') Rosemary Verey's famous laburnum walk

Recommended Pruning

Season Late winter or early spring

Recommended Forms Natural

Shaping Unnecessary

Maintaining Examine the tree in winter to look for damage. Thin it out. Other than this, golden chain trees require no pruning.

Restoring Unnecessary

Waterer hybrid laburnum
(*Laburnum* x *watereri* 'Vossii')

Scotch laburnum (*Laburnum alpinum*) flower panicle

Lagerstroemia indica

Crape Myrtle
LYTHRACEAE

This small, deciduous or evergreen tree is grown for its graceful form as well as the beauty of its flowers and peeling bark.

Hardiness Zones 7–9

Size 7 to 75 feet tall, 8 to 30 feet wide

Appearance The leaves of various species vary in shape, but are often oval or lance-shaped with smooth margins and usually grow opposite each other on the branch. The flowers are brightly colored and are clustered together in long, cone-shaped panicles. Colors range from whites to pink, rose, and purple, and the texture of the petals is crinkled, like crepe paper.

Exposure Full sun

Soil and Water Plant in moist, well-drained, moderately fertile soil.

Comments Where marginally hardy, plant crepe myrtles in a sheltered location to protect them from harsh winter winds. Of the many cultivars, *L. indica* 'Natchez' is a favorite because of its vigor. It has white blooms and reaches a height and width of 20 feet. *L. indica* 'Seminole' is smaller, reaching only 7 to 8 feet high and wide. It has vivid pink blooms with showy yellow centers. Both of these cultivars have some resistance to powdery mildew, a disease that can be quite damaging to crepe myrtles.

Crape myrtle (*Lagerstroemia indica* 'Natchez')

Crape myrtle
(*Lagerstroemia indica*
'Seminole')

Crape myrtle (*Lager-stroemia indica* 'Natchez')

Recommended Pruning

Season Late winter to early summer

Recommended Forms Natural

Shaping Unnecessary because plants have a naturally pleasing shape

Maintaining Pruning is not necessary to get good blooms, but flowers on unpruned trees tend to be smaller than those of trees that are pruned. To prune, cut back all branches in early spring before leaves appear. Check to see if any branches are damaged, too, and thin them out entirely. If you want to keep the plant shrub size, you can also cut back all branches to about 6 to 12 inches above the soil surface. These dwarfed plants will bloom, but they will be much smaller, of course.

Restoring Old crepe myrtles are as loved for their bark and graceful habit as for their flowers and are a valuable addition to the winter garden. But if you want to renovate a plant before it has reached this stage, cut it back to 6 to 12 inches from the soil. It will grow a number of branches over the growing season and bloom in midsummer, as normal.

Malus spp.

Crabapple
ROSACEAE

Crabapples put on spectacular shows in spring, when they bloom, and fall, when the leaves turn and then drop and ripened crabapples hang from the branches.

Hardiness Zones 4–8

Size 5 to 50 feet tall, 8 to 40 feet wide

Appearance Crabapple trees are variable in size. The leaves are alternate and are often toothed. Fragrant flowers in pink or white coat the branches in spring. They are soon followed by developing fruit. Ripe crabapples may be red, yellow, or orange. Most crabapples make good jellies and preserves but are too tart to eat raw. Unpicked, the fruit will persist into the winter on the branches and makes excellent bird food.

Exposure Full sun

Soil and Water Plant in moist, well-drained, moderately fertile soil with high humus levels.

Comments Like all members of the rose family, crabapples are susceptible to numerous insect pests and disease pathogens. If you live in a humid climate, take the time to search out a disease-resistant cultivar, such as the tea crabapple (*M. hupehensis*). Growing 40 feet tall and wide, this vigorous tree has pink buds that open to white blooms. Its crabapples are bright cherry red. Other resistant cultivars include 'Donald Wyman', 'Mary Potter', 'Adams', and 'Professor Sprenger'.

Crabapple
(*Malus* 'Snow Cloud')

Crabapple
(*Malus* 'Dorothea')

Crabapple
(*Malus sargentii*)

Crabapple
(*Malus* 'Donald Wyman')

Recommended Pruning

Season Late winter or early spring

Recommended Forms Natural or vase

Shaping Crabapples don't require the heavy pruning that apple trees do to bear fruit and, in fact, are more attractive if they are left to grow more naturally. However, if fruit is your goal, prune as directed on page 80 to form a vase shape.

Maintaining Every winter, examine your tree closely, and thin out any diseased or damaged wood. Thin out crossing or crowded growth as well, particularly if the tree has experienced any diseases.

Restoring Over the period of two or three years, thin out crowded wood, starting with watersprouts and vertical branches that do not bear. Then open up the center of the tree, thinning out old branches that are not bearing well. Finally, when the tree is the shape you want, go back to maintenance pruning.

Nyssa sylvatica

Black Gum
NYSSACEAE

Black gum trees are impressive shade trees with foliage that turns yellow, then brilliant orange, red, or purple in autumn.

Hardiness Zones 5–9

Size 25 to 70 feet tall, 25 to 30 feet wide

Appearance Leaves are oval, alternate, and smooth margined. The tree has inconspicuous flowers that produce copious amounts of nectar that bees love. Once pollinated, the flowers develop into clusters of small blue fruits. The fall foliage is truly spectacular and rivals the best of the red maples.

Exposure Full sun to partial shade

Soil and Water Grow in fertile, moist, well-drained soil with a pH that ranges from neutral to slightly acid; it does not do well in alkaline soils.

Comments The two most commonly grown black gum, or tupelo, trees are Chinese tupelo (*N. sinensis*) and the American native, black gum (*N. sylvatica*). Chinese tupelo is smaller than black gum, maturing to only 30 feet tall and wide. In contrast, black gum can reach 70 feet tall by 30 feet wide, and its bottom branches often droop to the ground.

Season Late winter or early spring

Recommended Forms Natural. In cold climates, the central leader sometimes has a hard time asserting dominance and the trees become multi-stemmed.

Shaping Unnecessary

Maintaining Check for damaged wood in winter, and thin it out.

Restoring Unnecessary

Black gum (*Nyssa sylvatica*)

5 Pruning Trees

Malus, Nyssa sylvatica

Black gum (*Nyssa sylvatica*) in fall

Black gum
(*Nyssa sylvatica*) berries in fall

Prunus spp.

Flowering Plums, Cherries, and Almonds
ROSACEAE

The ornamentals in this genus are grown for their flowers rather than their fruit, which tends to be small and only tasty if you're a bird.

Hardiness Zones 4–8

Size 5 to 50 feet tall, 5 to 30 feet wide

Appearance Leaves are usually toothed and oval to lance-shaped or rounded. Some species have dark purple leaves, but most are a mid-green color. Flowers range in color from whites and creams through pinks to reds, and can be single or double.

Exposure Full sun

Soil and Water Grow in moist, well-drained, fertile soil.

Comments Choose a cultivar grown in an area nursery for the best results. These trees are susceptible to the many rose diseases, so locally grown plants are generally the best adapted to your region. Flowering plums (*P. cerasifera*) are the earliest to bloom, and cultivars such as 'Thundercloud' have lovely purple leaves that persist through the season. Flowering cherries, such as the weeping *P. subhirtella* 'Pendula' with its single pink flowers or 'Pendula Plena Rosea' with double pink flowers, come next. Last to bloom, but still in very early spring, comes the flowering almond. The dwarf *P. glandulosa* is often grown in containers because it grows no more than 5 feet tall at the most.

Weeping Higan cherry
(*Prunus subhirtella* 'Pendula Plena Rosea')

Myrobalan plum
(*Prunus cerasifera* 'Thundercloud')

Flowering almond
(*Prunus glandulosa*)

Recommended Pruning

Season After bloom

Recommended Forms Natural

Shaping Aside from removing crossing and crowded wood, shaping is unnecessary.

Maintaining Each winter, examine trees for damage and disease and thin out affected branches. After blooming, cut back branches if necessary, and thin out old branches.

Restoring Begin by removing damaged or diseased growth, crossing branches, and about a third of the old and unproductive branches. The following two years, continue to cut out old growth, a third of it at a time. Remember that these trees are not as long-lived as many other trees; sometimes the easiest thing to do is remove the tree entirely.

Pyrus calleryana

Flowering Pear
ROSACEAE

Flowering pears are loved for their lavish display of blooms each spring, as well as their lovely fall foliage in shades of wine red or yellow.

Hardiness Zones 5–8

Size 50 feet tall, 50 feet wide

Appearance Leaves are alternate, dark green, glossy, and scalloped or toothed. Single white flowers with red anthers cover the tree in spring, and small brown or russet-colored fruit form after them.

Exposure Full sun or dappled shade

Soil and Water Grow in fertile, well-drained soil.

Comments 'Bradford' pear, which is probably the best known cultivar, has extremely narrow branching that makes the tree prone to a great deal of winter damage if you don't thin it out as it grows. The cultivars 'Capital', 'Cleveland Select', 'Redspire', and 'Whitehorse' all have more widely spaced branches.

Bradford pear
(*Pyrus calleryana* 'Bradford')

Season After flowering

Recommended Forms Natural

Shaping Unnecessary unless branches grow too closely together. In that case, thin them out when they first appear so the tree can withstand wind and winter snow and ice.

Maintaining Check for damaged or diseased wood each year, and thin it out while the plant is dormant or after flowering.

Restoring This can be a daunting challenge. If a great many closely spaced branches have been allowed to grow and the tree is suffering repeated winter damage, your best choice might be to remove it. If you want to try to save the tree, cut off a third of the excess growth at a time over the space of three years.

Bradford pear
(*Pyrus calleryana* 'Bradford')

Callery pear
(*Pyrus calleryana* 'Redspire')

5 Pruning Trees

Prunus, Pyrus calleryana

Tsuga spp.

Hemlock
PINACEAE

Loved for their graceful forms and long-lasting needles that keep the tree full, hemlocks are a favorite plant in Northern areas.

Hardiness Zones 3–7

Size 1 to 80 feet tall, 1 to 30 feet wide

Appearance These evergreen conifers have flattened leaves, or needles, that often have two silver bands on the undersides. The female cones are small, brown, and hang down. Male cones are tiny—no more than ¼ inch across—and are on the tips of lateral shoots.

Exposure Partial to full shade when young; eventually, the top of the tree grows tall enough to see sunlight.

Soil and Water Moist but well-drained, fertile, and humus-rich.

Comments Hemlocks are excellent specimen plants because of their striking good looks. Choose a weeping cultivar, such as *T. canadensis* 'Pendula', if you want a slow-growing tree that matures no higher than 5 feet tall. The Carolina hemlock is the best choice for Zones 6 and 7. It grows as tall as 65 feet and has the same good looks as northern species.

Canadian hemlock (*Tsuga canadensis*)

Carolina hemlock
(*Tsuga caroliniana*)

Canadian hemlock
(*Tsuga canadensis*) fruits (cones)

Recommended Pruning

Season After its main growth spurt in spring

Recommended Forms Natural

Shaping Unnecessary unless you are training it as a hedge. In this case, shape it when young by cutting back to encourage bottom growth, and trim it every year in early to mid-summer.

Maintaining Check for damaged wood every year, and prune it out.

Restoring Unnecessary

Ulmus parvifolia

Chinese Elm
ULMACEAE

This lovely tree resembles the American elm in habit and deserves to be as widely planted as it once was.

Hardiness Zones 5–9

Size 40 to 50 feet tall, 25 to 40 feet wide

Appearance Leaves are elliptic, toothed, glossy, and a mid-green color. They turn yellow or red in autumn. The tree bears tiny red flowers in late summer and fall, and winged, green fruit follow them.

Exposure Full sun or partial shade

Soil and Water Grow in well-drained soil of moderate fertility. Plants can tolerate urban soils that have low organic matter and nutrients.

Comments The cultivar 'Allee' ('Elmer 11') has a form that resembles the round-topped American elm. The gray-colored bark of Chinese elm is highly decorative, peeling in patches to reveal orange wood beneath. The weeping forms, such as 'Sempervirens', are excellent specimen trees for the yard because its habit is so graceful.

Recommended Pruning

Season Late winter to early spring

Recommended Forms Natural

Shaping Unnecessary

Maintaining Check for damaged wood each year, and prune it out.

Restoring Unnecessary

Chinese elm
(*Ulmus parvifolia*)

Chinese elm
(*Ulmus parvifolia*)

American elm (*Ulmus americana*)

Weeping Chinese elm (*Ulmus parvifolia* 'Sempervirens')

Tsuga, Ulmus parvifolia

pruning fruiting plants

Pruning Fruiting Plants

Pruning fruiting plants—trees, bushes, or vines—intimidates most people at first because it seems so irrevocable. Many people worry that they will cut off a necessary branch, leaving their tree without a proper framework. But the fearful should take heart. If you pay attention to what you are doing, it is unlikely that you will cut off an important branch, and even if you did, trees have the capacity to grow more than one limb in roughly the same area. Remember, too, that if pruning required the IQ of a genius or a sixth sense about plants, there would be far fewer apples in the world. Pruning, despite its importance to the tree, is not difficult to learn to do successfully. But pruning does require some thought. Before you begin, think about the purposes of your pruning task, the ways that the tree will react to various cuts, and the best timing for your pruning operation.

Purposes of Pruning. Good pruning strengthens the tree and makes it more productive. When the tree is young, you prune to give it a strong framework of scaffold branches that are positioned to allow both light and air into the center of the tree.

As the tree matures, you prune to keep the tree from growing too large; to maintain a balance between shoot and fruit production; to remove weak, damaged, or diseased growth; to allow air and light to reach all parts of the tree; and to stimulate new growth where you want it.

The Consequences of Pruning. As explained earlier, plant growth is regulated by chemical compounds called auxins that promote growth at the tip of the stem but inhibit the development of growth below it. This effect is what prevents a plant from growing a new branch at every bud. When you are pruning off the tip of a stem, which removes the area where the auxin is being produced, you will be making a decision about where you want the next branch to develop. For example, pinching off the very tip of the branch encourages branching just below the pinched area.

Winter is the perfect time to study the form of your trees and decide how best to prune them.

Tree Anatomy

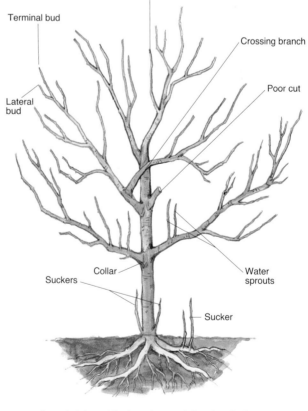

Pruning is much easier once you can identify the various parts of a tree. Though each tree is different, you'll see many of these structures on your own tree.

- Vertical branch that will not bear fruit
- Terminal bud
- Crossing branch
- Poor cut
- Lateral bud
- Collar
- Water sprouts
- Suckers
- Sucker

Prune to bring out the best characteristics of each of your trees and minimize their weak points.

When you shorten a stem by cutting back by a third, several of the buds just below the cut will begin to grow. To promote even more vigorous growth of a bud very low on the branch, prune off two-thirds of the stem. In general, the buds nearest the cut make the most vigorous upright growth, while those that grow lower down on the stem make wider angles. The bud that develops nearest the tip of the stem will eventually become a dominant branch and produce auxins to inhibit the growth of buds below it. All pruning cuts used to cut back stems are referred to as heading cuts.

Thinning cuts are those that totally remove growth. Use thinning cuts to prune off weak or poorly positioned branches, water sprouts, and sprouts from the rootstock. When you remove a branch along a stem, the tip of the stem grows even more vigorously,

and latent buds are less likely to develop. If you want the stem to form a branch in a different spot than the branch that you pruned, remove the site of auxin production by heading back the stem an appropriate distance, as discussed in the Smart Tip.

Fruit seeds also produce auxins that affect subsequent growth. If too many auxins are present, such as when the tree has produced a large crop, far fewer flower buds will sprout for the next year's crop. This is why some trees bear heavily only in alternate years.

Thinning, or pruning off, the developing fruit not only evens out production from one year to the next, but it also increases the size of the remaining fruit. It is best to thin the fruit twice, once just after the blossoms have dropped and again just after the June fruit drop. As a general rule,

allow a space two to three times the size of the mature fruit between the fruit you leave on the tree.

Timing. Most heading-cut pruning on apples, pears, and quinces is done in late winter or very early spring, while the plant is still dormant.

Tree Shapes

The shape of your tree will be determined in large part by the type of tree it is. In general, dwarf and semidwarf trees are best pruned as vase or modified central-leader trees, while standard trees can be pruned as central-leader or modified central-leader trees.

Central-leader pruning depends on well-placed scaffold branches to allow light into the center.

Modified central-leader pruning requires you to cut out the central leader after the fourth or fifth scaffold branch grows.

Vase, or open, pruning is done by cutting back the leader to form a completely open center.

When the tree comes out of dormancy, the lack of auxin production at the headed-back stem tips causes lateral buds to grow vigorously.

In contrast, very little to no dormant pruning is done on peaches and nectarines because it promotes early blooming. The first defense against frost damage to these trees is to wait until the tree is already in bloom to make heading cuts. If done at this time, the tree still responds by producing new growth along branches that have been headed back.

Pruning in summer reduces rather than stimulates regrowth. You can use this to your advantage when you are making thinning cuts to bring light into the center of the tree or to remove unwanted growth. Heading cuts done in midsummer can have the effect of stimulating the formation of flower buds rather than those that will grow into shoots. Growers use this method to promote maximum fruiting on espalier-trained trees, as discussed on page 86.

Preparing for Pruning. Before taking so much as the first cut on your tree, learn about its natural growth habits and the shape that most growers give it. As illustrated opposite, the three most common ways to prune and train fruit trees are central leader, modified central leader, and vase, or open, shape. In general, dwarf and semidwarf trees are pruned to a vase or modified central leader, while standards are frequently pruned to a modified central leader or central leader. Specific pruning instructions for each fruit tree are given in the directory on pages 87–107.

Once, gardeners were advised to prune off all the branches of a young tree when they planted it to allow roots to grow before leaves did. However, current knowledge about plant growth means that growers now give very different instructions.

If the tree is "feathered," meaning that it already has some branches, plant it, and then look carefully at it. Your goal is to retain any well-positioned branches. Pruning, even if done when the tree is dormant, stimulates growth near the cuts but sets back the tree's overall growth. Ideally, the bottom branch will be about 2 feet above the soil surface and will be growing at an angle of at least 40 degrees from the trunk. If as many as two other branches are spaced 6 to 8 inches apart on the trunk, grow or can be trained to grow at a 40-degree or greater angle, and are positioned in a neat spiral around the trunk, you'll want to retain them too.

Before pruning. The branches of this peach tree are too closely spaced and prevent light from reaching the center of the tree.

After pruning. The same peach tree has been opened up so light can reach the center, eliminating weak or misplaced growth.

6 Pruning Fruiting Plants

Head back each of the retained branches to a few inches, always cutting just above an outward-facing bud, unless the tree is a dwarf that you are growing in a trellised system. Thin branches that are growing too closely to a desired branch, that do not help to form a spiral around the trunk, or that grow at such a strong angle that they cannot be trained to a more horizontal position. Head back the central leader to about 3 feet from the soil surface.

In the second year, pruning is dictated by the tree's form. If you are growing a central-leader tree, head back the leader again so that a new tier of scaffold branches will develop; thin out undesirable growth; and head back the branches. Cut back about a third of the previous year's growth from the central leader.

With a modified central-leader tree, cut back the central leader to just above the fourth scaffold branch. If the tree lacks this branch, head back the central leader. By the third season, there will be enough branches for you to cut back the central leader. Head back the branches you have decided to keep, and then thin out any undesirable growth.

With trees with open centers, the central leader is usually removed during the second year. By this time, the trees usually have grown the three branches that form the vase shape. Thin undesirable growth.

You can widen branch angles in several ways. Insert a wooden toothpick between a developing branch and the leader to force the branch into a more horizontal form, or weight the branch with wooden clothespins. You can hang weights from larger branches or tie these branches to weights on the ground.

Pruning Mature Trees. Trees require pruning at all growth stages. Good pruning helps to maintain the health of the tree, keeps it a manageable size, and promotes top-quality fruit every year. Make it a habit to cut out diseased branches while the tree is dormant, unless it is a peach or nectarine. (See "Pruning Guidelines," opposite, for specific instructions.) As the tree ages, you'll make most of your thinning cuts—many of which can be done in summer—toward the top of the tree and most of the heading cuts toward the bottom.

Use a small pruning saw to cut branches that are no thicker than ½ in. thick.

Dormant pruning on a warm winter day can be a highlight of the gardening season.

Pruning Guidelines

- Prune only as much as necessary to create the desired shape, to allow light into the center, and to keep the tree healthy and bearing well.
- When pruning a dormant tree, wait to prune until the wood has thawed in the morning sun.
- Use only appropriate tools, and sharpen them before every use. Sterilize tools with a 10 percent laundry bleach solution after every cut on a diseased tree.
- When pruning off diseased or insect-infested growth, cut back the branch at least 6 inches beyond the site of the problem.
- Remove and destroy all diseased and insect-infested wood. Do not leave it near the tree or compost it.
- Cut all branches just below the collar. (See the illustration on page 81.) When pruning branches back, make the cut above an outward-facing bud.
- Do not use tree paint to protect wounds.
- Make clean cuts with sharp tools.
- Angle all cuts so excess moisture drips off, discouraging organisms that thrive in high-moisture conditions.
- Prune peaches and nectarines only when they are actively growing, not when they are dormant. With your finger, rub off undesirable buds during the growing season so that you won't have to prune them off the following year.
- Prune off diseased growth immediately. If you wait until the tree is dormant, the problem can worsen.

Thin out developing fruit if they look crowded, left. It's better to have fewer good fruit than lots of diseased fruit. When pruning branches, cut above an outward-facing bud, below.

Spurs form best on lateral branches pruned back to the top flower bud.

Fruit grows from the buds left on the branch. A spur will remain after harvesting.

Additional spurs will form each year. They will be just below the fruits that grow.

After a few years spurs will become too crowded. Prune out older ones.

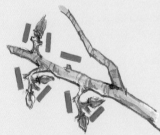

Thin the spurs as necessary in late winter or early spring every year.

6 Pruning Fruiting Plants

Espaliered Fruit Trees

An espaliered fruit tree can be the centerpiece of your yard. These formal designs also have the advantage of ensuring that trees are extremely well maintained and that the fruits are large and healthy.

The most appropriate trees for espaliers are cultivars that bear on spurs. Espalier designs dictate that you remove many stem tips and some lateral branches, the sites where trees without spurs flower and fruit. Because spurs grow all along the branches, espalier training does not cut the yields of spur-bearers. Experienced growers recommend that you espalier dwarfs or small semidwarf trees because their less-vigorous growth means less pruning and training.

The first step toward establishing an espaliered tree is choosing where to grow it. Many of these trees are planted and trained against walls. A wall gives excellent support for the training wires and can protect the plant from harsh winds. Stone or masonry walls store enough heat to moderate temperatures, as well. As long as you remember to protect blooms from late hard frosts, this temperature moderating quality can work in your favor for marginally hardy cultivars.

Some commercial orchardists have begun to put in acres of intensively grown dwarf or semidwarf cultivars that are trained on wires in an espalier fashion. A series of trees is grown on long rows of the trellis system, spaced far enough apart to allow air to circulate between trees. Even though this training system is more labor-intensive than growing normal modified central-leader trees, the increased yields and consistent fruit quality make it economically practical.

How to Prune Espaliers. Pruning for espalier systems differs from other types of pruning in two important ways. First, the only branches you retain are those you can train along the horizontal supports, and second, late summer or early fall pruning is as intense as dormant pruning.

During the first season, allow three or four branches to grow along the supports, tying them into place as they grow. Small shoots will grow from these branches during the summer. In the late summer or early fall, after the bark on these shoots has turned brown and the bases of the shoots have become woody, cut them back to retain three leaves beyond the basal cluster of leaves. In future years, when you will prune some stubs that you created the year before, prune to one leaf above the basal cluster.

When the tree is dormant, prune the fruiting spurs so that the fruit will be well spaced. If any of the shoots you pruned the previous fall or late summer have regrown, prune them back again. Use this time to head back the horizontal branches as well.

Espaliered trees add a note of elegance to any yard.

This apple cordon has been trained along a fence to form a simple espalier.

Citrus spp.

Citrus trees, including orange, grapefruit, lemon, and lime
RUTACEAE

Citrus tree
(*Citrus* spp.)

If you live in a frost-free climate, citrus trees are a fabulous addition to your yard. Further north, grow them in containers and move them inside when the weather is cool.

Hardiness Zones 9–11

Size 5 to 35 feet tall, 8 to 35 feet wide

Appearance The leaves of these evergreens are glossy and dark green with a smooth edge. Flowers, which appear in midwinter and intermittently through the spring and summer, are intensely fragrant, white, and waxy-looking.

Exposure Full sun, but can tolerate afternoon shade in extremely hot locations

Soil and Water Plant in well-drained soil with higher fertility and moisture levels during the summer.

Comments Citrus trees do not require a pollinator, so you can grow just one with great success. Always buy citrus trees from a local nursery, one that grows the plants it sells, because the rootstocks of citrus are chosen to do well in particular areas.

If you are growing a containerized plant in a northern area, set it into a protected spot during summer, and bring it inside long before the first frost—when evenings just begin to get cool. Place it in a window where it can receive bright light for the whole day, and supplement the lighting with a high-quality, full spectrum grow light. They fruit best with a daylength from 10 to 12 hours during the winter, so set the lights to be sure they are getting good light for this amount of time.

The two major kinds of oranges are navel, which is best for eating fresh, and Valencia, which is best for juice. One of the most interesting navels is 'Cara Cara', with pink flesh and excellent flavor. If you are looking for an early ripening navel, grow 'Fukomoto', a Japanese cultivar. Valencia oranges tend to have a lot of seeds, but a relatively new cultivar, 'Midknight' is seedless and still has excellent flavor and high juice content. Blood oranges are just becoming popular in the U.S. Three types are available—Moro, Sanguinelli, and Tarocco. Check with local nurseries to see which is best adapted to your climate.

Tangerines are actually Mandarin oranges. There are many cultivars, but some of the favorites include 'Owari Satsuma', adapted to southern California conditions, and 'Florida Honey', an East Coast cultivar.

'Eureka', and 'Meyer' are common lemons, with 'Eureka' being the one you usually see in the grocery store. These are a treat to grow and are generally easier than oranges. 'Meyer' lemon is the most cold-hardy, tolerating temperatures as low as 26°F. The most unusual lemon is the Ponderosa, which is sometimes called the "football" lemon because it can weigh more than two pounds. It is actually a citron-lemon hybrid rather than a true lemon.

If you grow your own limes, you can savor them when they are truly ripe—when they turn yellow! Green limes are a marketing strategy to distinguish them from lemons. Interesting limes include Keffir limes, which have leaves and flowers that are used in Middle Eastern cooking; the small Key lime that's common in South Florida and is used in the famous key lime pie; and the Palestine Sweet lime that is truly sweet.

Grapefruits are magnificent trees that bear huge numbers of fruit. 'Ruby Red' is a favorite and may be grown on various rootstocks to suit your particular climate. 'Marsh' is an equally popular white cultivar.

Recommended Pruning

Season Midspring to midsummer

Recommended Forms Natural

Shaping Unnecessary

Maintaining Examine each year to check for damage or poorly positioned growth. Remove damage when you see it, but wait until spring to remove poorly positioned growth. If removing frost-damaged wood, wait until growth resumes so you can see the extent of the damage. Lemons are the only citrus that requires diligent pruning; every two years, head back overly long branches to keep the tree in bounds and the fruit easy to pick. Remember that citrus flower and fruit on current growth. If the tree looks as though it is bearing too many fruit at once, thin them out when they are small.

Restoring This is rarely necessary, but if you inherit a tree with a lot of growth in the center, gradually remove it over the space of several years. Remove any suckers growing from the roots, too.

Malus spp.

Apple
ROSACEAE

What could be better than an apple picked from a tree in your yard and eaten on the spot?

Hardiness Zones 3–9

Size 8 to 30 feet tall, 8 to 40 feet wide

Appearance Leaves of most apple cultivars are shiny and dark green. They have a pointed tip and serrated edges.

Exposure Full sun, preferably on a north-facing slope so blooms don't open when frosts are still occurring

Soil and Water Well-drained soil that is moderately fertile with a pH of 6.5 to 6.8. Requires fertilization with fully finished compost each year to maintain good health.

Comments Most cultivars require a pollinator; check with your supplier for an appropriate pollinating species when you buy. Apples can be difficult because of the many pests and diseases that attack them. Buy trees only from local growers, and choose resistant cultivars; trying to combat problems can take all the joy out of growing your own fruit.

Disease-resistant cultivars are becoming more and more common these days. In humid areas, look for resistance to apple scab, powdery mildew, cedar-apple rust, and fire blight. 'Redfree', 'Priscilla', 'Freedom' and 'Liberty' all have good to superior resistance to these diseases and are also known for their excellent flavor and appearance.

Pest-resistant cultivars include 'Sunrise' and 'Pioneer Mac', both of which are strongly resistant to common foliage and fruit pests. 'Goldrush' tests as very resistant to foliage pests, while 'Pristine' tests best for resistance to fruit pests.

Apple
(*Malus* spp.)

Recommended Pruning

Season Late winter and early spring

Recommended Forms Depends on cultivar and growth situation. Apples will grow as central leader, modified central leader, vase, or espaliered types, and some novelty cultivars are bred to grow as single columns.

Shaping After planting or in the following spring, choose future scaffold branches and thin the others. Scaffold branches should be growing at about a 50-degree angle from the central leader. Prune off any branches growing about 4 inches from the ground. Also prune off any downward-facing branches because fruit growing on them won't see enough light to ripen well. Head back the leader and branch tips. The upper branches should always be shorter than the lower ones so that light can reach the fruit.

Maintaining Examine the tree for crossing growth, as well as damaged or diseased wood, and prune off. Remember to prune to an outward-facing bud when you head back a branch. Do this in summer. As the tree ages, be diligent about removing both suckers growing from the base of the tree and watersprouts. Thin both fruit and old spurs for the best production. Spur-bearing trees tend to grow about 6 to 12 inches a year and non-spur-bearing trees grow from 1 to 2 feet a year. Head back the leader and top scaffold branches if the tree threatens to grow too large.

Restoring Restore the tree over the course of several years. On a standard tree with a central leader, begin by cutting back the leader; then cut the upper scaffold limbs about 2 feet shorter than you cut the central leader. If it is a dwarf, you may not need to shorten the central leader or scaffold limbs. If it is pruned to be a vase, head back all the top branches as if they were central leaders. Then prune out or head back horizontal wood in the upper third of the tree. The following spring, new branches will have grown. In most cases, you will remove almost all of this growth—you are trying to open the tree up to see more light, after all. In the third spring, head back the leader and top scaffold branches again, and remove excess growth on the interior of the tree and waterspouts. Leave lower limbs that are healthy but thin, and cut back to leave an upward-facing shoot at the ends of these limbs. In the fourth spring, thin out about half of the new growth at the top of the tree. By this time, the lower limbs are beginning to grow. In the fifth year, you can resume normal pruning for the tree.

Prunus avium

Sweet Cherry
ROSACEAE

A cherry tree in the yard invites every bird for miles around. Net the tree if you want to compete with the birds.

Hardiness Zones 5–9

Size 6 to 35 feet tall, 8 to 40 feet wide

Appearance Leaves are pointed and dark green with serrated edges.

Exposure Full sun

Soil and Water Well-drained, deep, and moderately fertile. They require a top dressing of fully finished compost every spring.

Comments Many sweet cherries need another species nearby for pollination. Check with your supplier for compatible cultivars. 'Bing' cherries are relatively easy to grow but may crack badly after a rainstorm when they are just about ripe. 'BentonT' has moderate to good crack resistance. 'Hudson' and 'Lapin' are both crack resistant, late cherries that are quite firm. 'Cavalier' and 'Viva' are both early cultivars with moderate crack resistance.

 'Rainier' cherries have yellow skin with a red blush and yellow flesh. They have extremely high sugar levels and fine-textured flesh.

 A few sweet cherries are self-fruitful, meaning they don't need a pollinator, although they do fruit better with one. 'Sweetheart' is a self-fruitful cultivar that is quite late and well loved for its flavor and firm texture. 'Stella' has spotty production unless it is pollinated. You will get fruit if you plant it alone, but you will get better yields from it with another cherry nearby. To get reliable production from a self-pollinating tree, grow 'WhiteGoldT', a new cultivar that was bred from 'Stella' and a cherry named 'Emperor Francis'.

Sweet cherry
(*Prunus avium*)

Recommended Pruning

Season Late winter or early spring and summer

Recommended Forms Standard cherries are tall trees and are often pruned to a central leader or modified central leader. They resent hard pruning, so the only sweet cherries to be given an open, or vase, shape are dwarfs or those growing in intensely managed commercial orchards.

Shaping The year after planting, choose the scaffold branches you will keep and thin out the others. Head back the scaffold branches to encourage branching. In the following year, do this again. Choose your scaffold branches carefully, and be certain not to choose branches forming opposite from each other because they can become quite heavy when they are bearing and split the trunk. Once the tree begins bearing, thin more aggressively so that light reaches all portions of the tree's interior.

Maintaining Fruit forms on one to ten-year-old spurs, so it's important to thin out old spurs to make room for new ones. Check each year for damage, disease, and poorly positioned growth, and thin out as necessary. If you cut back only a portion of a branch, prune to an outward-facing bud so that the new growth doesn't crowd the center. You do not need to thin the fruit, but you do need to thin spurs that are nearing their 10-year maturity.

Restoring Restore cherry trees gradually. On a standard tree with a central leader or modified central leader, begin by cutting back the leader; then cut the upper scaffold limbs about 2 feet shorter than you cut the leader. If the tree is pruned to be a vase, head back all the top branches as if they were central leaders. Then, for all trees, prune out or head back horizontal wood in the upper third of the tree. The following spring, look at the tree. New branches will have grown. Choose which branches to retain and which to thin out entirely. In most cases, you will remove almost all of this growth—you are trying to open the tree up to see more light, after all. In the third spring, head back the leader and upper scaffold branches again, and remove excess growth in the interior of the tree. Leave lower limbs that are healthy, but cut back to leave an upward-facing shoot at the ends of these limbs. In the fourth spring, thin out about half of the new growth at the top of the tree. By this time, the lower limbs will be growing well because of the light they are receiving. Remove crowded or crossing branches. Otherwise, let these limbs develop. In the fifth year, you can resume normal pruning for the tree.

Prunus domestica, P. salicina

Plum
ROSACEAE

Plums make lovely garden trees that give you fragrant flowers in spring, delicious fruit in summer, lovely leaf color in autumn, and a graceful habit that's visible in winter.

Hardiness Zones European: 4–9; Japanese: 6–10

Size European, 1 to 20 feet tall, 10 to 20 feet wide; Japanese, 10 to 20 feet tall, 10 to 20 feet wide

Appearance Leaves are glossy and dark green, with pointed tips. In some cultivars, there is a purple undertone to the green. They turn yellow in autumn. Flowers are so beautiful that many purely ornamental plums—without edible fruit—are grown in yards and landscapes all over the world. Fortunately, fruiting plums have the same kind of pink or white flowers that form in clusters in early spring.

Exposure Full sun, ideally on a north slope so late frosts don't injure the blossoms

Plum (*P. domestica*)

Soil and Water Grow in well-drained soil with high fertility. European plums tolerate heavy clay soils, but Japanese plums prefer a lighter, more sandy soil.

Comments Almost all Japanese plums and many European plums require a pollinator, so ask at your nursery about appropriate species. European and Japanese plums are different in their fruiting habits. European plums fruit on 2 to 6-year-old spurs and Japanese plums fruit on spurs a year or more old. Remember to thin out old spurs when they get crowded to keep your tree producing well.

Recommended Pruning

Season Both dormant and summer pruning are necessary.

Recommended Forms European plums should be pruned to a modified central-leader form and Japanese plums to an open, or vase, shape.

Shaping (for central-leader and modified central-leader trees). After planting, head back the leader so it's about 2 to 3 feet above the soil surface and just above a bud. Wait until the new growth is about 3 or 4 inches long; then choose your first set of scaffold branches. Because you'll want them to have about a 60-degree angle from the leader, you may have to use spreaders to widen the angles.

The following early spring, while the tree is still dormant, head back the leader to about 30 inches above the topmost scaffold branch. That summer, select additional scaffold branches, and leave an 18-inch "light slot" between the first and second whorls of scaffold branches. Each year, follow the same routine.

For open-center, or vase, trees, head back the whip once the buds begin to swell to about 2 to 3 feet above the soil surface. After shoots grow to about 3 or 4 inches long, select the shoots that will become scaffolds. The lowest one should be no closer to the ground than 2 or 3 feet.

In early spring the next year, head back the scaffold branches to encourage lateral branches on them. Repeat this during the late dormant period for the next two years. In the summer, remove undesirable growth as soon as it is 4 to 6 inches long.

Maintaining For central-leader trees, head back the central leader, and thin out damaged or diseased growth during the dormant period. Cut back the laterals at this time to maintain the pyramid shape. During summer, thin crowded growth. Once the tree is at the desired size, head back the lateral branches and the central leader each year. You can do this by cutting back into 2-year-old wood, to a shoot growing on the side. This shoot should be about the same diameter as the branch or leader that you are heading back. Thin out vertical growth each summer.

For open-center trees, once the tree starts bearing, prune in the late dormant season to remove upright growth on the scaffolds and trunk. Remove all damaged, dead, and diseased wood as well.

Restoring Restore trees gradually, removing about a third of the excess growth at a time, starting with the upright watersprouts and dead, damaged, or diseased growth, as well as a third of the excess growth at the top of the tree.

Prunus persica;
P. persica var. nucipersica

Peach, Nectarine
ROSACEAE

The pleasure your family will get from having a peach or nectarine tree will more than make up for the care it requires.

Hardiness Zones 5–9

Size 4 to 20 feet tall, 6 to 25 feet wide

Appearance Leaves are long and pointed, and droop gracefully in clusters from the branches. They turn yellow in the autumn. The early spring-blooming flowers are pink and may be single or double. Like all members of the rose family, they have prominent stamens.

Exposure Full sun in a protected area that faces north, ideally a slope so that frost rolls down and away

Soil and Water Plant in well-drained soil with high fertility. They thrive in sandy soils and need fertilization with fully finished compost. They may require extra nitrogen, calcium, and phosphorus, so supplement with 1 cup of alfalfa meal, 1 cup of gypsum, and 1 cup of rock phosphate; spread it evenly over the root area before you spread the compost if the trees begin to look less than spectacular.

Comments Most cultivars of both nectarines and peaches are self-fruitful, so you do not need another species. Buy plants only from local nurseries that grow the trees on site. This is particularly important in the south because both types of trees have chilling hour requirements, meaning that they both must experience a certain number of hours when the temperature is between 32 and 45°F. Different cultivars have different requirements. The nursery will know the average number of chilling hours your area receives as well as the cultivars that do well in these conditions. In general, nectarines require from 800 to 1,200 hours and peaches require from 200 to 1,200 hours.

These fruits ripen after you pick them, although they taste best when allowed to nearly ripen on the tree. Once they are fully ripe, you can hold them in the refrigerator, but if cooled before the sugars have developed and they are truly ripe, they will never be very sweet. And even though they will continue to ripen after they are picked, that ripening is only a matter of becoming softer, not becoming sweeter. So it's advisable to leave them on the tree until they truly are ripe. You determine this with your nose—ripe peaches and nectarines have an unmistakable perfume.

There are enormous numbers of both peach and nectarine cultivars, and they vary according to their time of ripening as well as flavor and structure. Both can be freestone or cling. "Freestone" means that the pit falls away

Peach
(*P. persica*)

from the flesh easily, and "cling" means that it clings to it.

Most nectarines are freestone. However, some, such as 'Independence' are semi-cling. 'Summer Beaut' is a fairly early nectarine that tolerates cold winters well. Both flavor and appearance are excellent, and the tree is known for producing large crops. 'Mericrest' is the hardiest nectarine. It produces fruit in the middle of the season, so you'll get them before frost.

White nectarines are becoming more popular. Of these, 'Arctic Rose' is known for its firm, very sweet fruit with a deep rose-colored skin. 'Arctic Jay' also has deep rose skin and fruit with good flavor. It is hardy to Zone 6, but is quite prone to bacterial leaf spot disease.

Recommended Pruning

Season Just before the buds open and in summer

Recommended Forms Central leader and modified central leader for standard trees; vase or open shape for dwarf trees.

Shaping See Plums, opposite. The only difference is one of timing. Do the pruning operations specified for the late dormant season for plums just a bit later for peaches and nectarines—right before the buds open. Other than that difference, all techniques are the same.

Maintaining See the directions for Plums, opposite. Again, notice that the timing is slightly different. Rather than pruning in the late dormant period, wait until just before the buds open. Both peaches and nectarines can set too many fruit. Thin out developing fruit if they look crowded. It's better to have fewer good fruit than lots of diseased fruit.

Restoring See directions for Plums, opposite, and be sure to wait to prune until just before the buds open.

Pruning Fruiting Shrubs

Most fruiting shrubs do not require intense pruning to remain healthy and productive. Bushes grow by developing new stems from the crown of the plant every year. Individual branches are not long lived, but the new growth every year means that the bush itself may be. As a gardener, your job is to remove old or diseased growth to make way for healthy new stems. In the case of fruiting shrubs, you'll also want to open up the center of the plant so that light and air can penetrate to the inside.

Fruiting shrubs vary in response to pruning, however. Even though you have the option of doing nothing more than thinning old growth from all of them, some respond to more-specialized pruning by giving higher yields of healthier fruit than might be possible if you simply let them grow as bushes.

After planting, there are two ways to handle a fruiting shrub. In the case of blueberries, cranberries, and serviceberries (*Amelanchier*), the best advice is to treat them as bushes and do as little pruning as possible. Thin out weak branches, and head back any damaged wood, always cutting to an outside bud. As the spring progresses, some of these bushes will bloom.

Thin old canes by cutting flush with the soil surface. Do this work when the plants are dormant.

Pruning Guidelines

Fruiting shrubs are among the hardest working plants in the landscape. They provide year-round structure and deliver a delicious crop. Some fruiting shrubs are pretty enough to be used as specimens, while others make good hedges.

Common	Botanical	Zones	Soil Needs	Pruning Needs	Fruiting Time	Pollinators Required
Blueberry, lowbush	*Vaccinium angustifolium*	3 to 8	Acid	Light	Late summer/fall	Yes
Blueberry, rabbiteye	*Vaccinium ashei*	6 to 9	Acid	Light	Late summer/fall	Yes
Blueberry, highbush	*Vaccinium corymbosum*	4 to 8	Acid	Light	Late summer/fall	Yes
Blueberry, half-high	*Vaccinium corymbosum*	4 to 7	Acid	Light	Late summer/fall	Yes
Cranberry	*Vaccinium macrocarpon*	2 to 6	Acid, moist	Light	Fall	No
Currant, black	*Ribes nigrum*	3 to 6	High fertility	Moderate	Summer	Yes
Currant, red & white	*Ribes silvestre & R. petraeum*	3 to 6	High fertility	Moderate	Summer	No
Elderberry, American	*Sambucus canadensis*	2 to 9	Deep, drained	Light	Late summer/fall	Yes
Gooseberry, European	*Ribes uva-crispa*	3 to 7	High fertility	Moderate	Summer	No
Gooseberry, American	*Ribes hirtellum*	3 to 7	High fertility	Moderate	Summer	No
Jostaberry	*Ribes x nidigrolaria*	3 to 7	High fertility	Moderate	Summer	No
Serviceberry	*Amelanchier* spp.	3 to 8	Well-drained	Light	Summer	No

Even though it may be hard to do so, pinch off the flowers so that the plant can put all of its strength into root and shoot growth.

Shrubs are always pruned when they are dormant. After the first year, thin out weak or damaged growth and any branches that crowd the center of the plant. Otherwise, wait to do major pruning until the third or fourth year.

Highbush and half-high blueberries fruit on stems one to four years old. After that, productivity declines. Thin all 5-year-old stems, cutting at the soil level. To keep the plant sturdy, head back all drooping stems and those that are less than ¼ inch thick. Always cut just above an outside bud or branch. Thin out twiggy growth and stems that crowd the center of the plant. If the plant has more than five fruit buds on each fruiting stem, head the stems back so that they don't carry more than this number. Even though the number of fruits will be fewer, the size of the berries will be larger.

Rabbiteye blueberries are pruned in a similar fashion except that you probably won't need to head back fruiting stems because these plants are unlikely to have too many fruit buds on a stem. Also, rabbiteye plants are generally more vigorous and robust than highbush and half-high blueberries and usually do not need as many stems headed back or thinned.

Lowbush blueberries form new shoots from underground rhizomes, as well as from buds on the branches. They will also form roots from the nodes of stems that lie on the ground. They fruit on one-year-old wood, and the biggest and best fruits come from shoots growing from the rhizomes rather than from aboveground wood. Prune to stimulate this kind of fruiting. The third year after planting, cut half of your plants to the ground while they are dormant. The half you didn't prune will set fruit that year. During the next dormant period, cut all the stems to the ground on the half of the plants that you allowed to fruit that year. Alternate pruning in this way to keep your bushes healthy and bearing well.

Pruning Ribes Species. Currants, gooseberries, and josta-berries can be handled a number of ways. You have a choice of growing them as bushes, or "stools"; on a single stem or "leg"; and, except for black currants, as espaliered cordons.

Pruning *Ribes* Species

Pruning *Ribes* species is very straightforward if you simply allow them to grow as bushes. As long as you keep up with this minimal work, the plants will continue to thrive and produce abundant fruit.

1. In the third to fifth year, depending on the species, thin out the oldest stems.

2. The following year, repeat this process, always removing the stems that have borne fruit the longest.

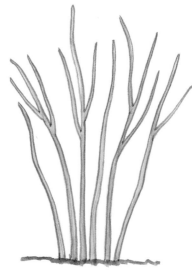

3. By continuing in this way, your plant will always have young, vital, fruitbearing stems.

Growing these plants as bushes is by far the easiest alternative. If you are a beginning fruit grower, this is probably the best choice you can make unless your landscape design demands a more formal-looking system. To grow the plants as stools, cut back all of the stems to two to four buds above the soil level just after planting. During the first year, the plant will develop branches from each of these buds, as well as new branches that originate underground.

When the plant is dormant, thin out any weak growth, and then thin the strong, upright growth so that only six or seven stems remain. Thin stems by cutting just at or slightly below soil level. In subsequent years you will repeat this dormant pruning, but in the third year you must thin out all the 3-year-old stems.

Pruning on a Leg. To prune plants to grow on a leg, rub off all the buds on the bottom 6 inches or so of the central stem. Prune the plant during the dormant season almost as you would if it were a tree you were growing in a central-leader design. First develop four or five branches as a permanent framework; then head back the lateral branches that form on the framework when you prune each year. Thin out weak branches and twiggy growth in the center of the plant each year, and remove branches that are more than 3 years old.

In England, gardeners often train currants and gooseberries to cordons. As with other espalier systems, it is best to set up the trellis before you plant. Because you'll be tying the branches to lathing strips lashed to the wires, you should determine how many stems you're going to allow to develop beforehand. Prune off the unwanted growth, and tie the stems to the lathing strips as they grow.

Pruning to a Leg

Currants, gooseberries, and jostaberries all thrive when they are grown as a "leg," or on a single stem that you train to act as a trunk. This method is easy to do, but takes more time each year than growing plants as simple bushes.

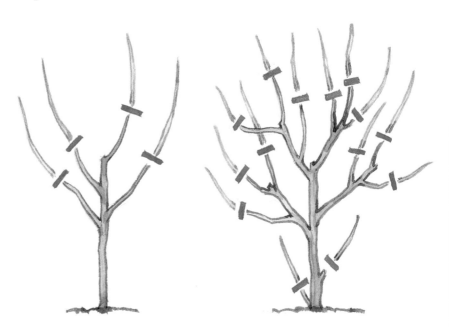

1. After developing the central stem and allowing four good branches to grow, head them back.

2. Each year, when the plant is dormant, head back the branches and remove any branches from the trunk.

3. To promote good growth, head back the tips of laterals on which fruit forms each year.

4. Remove 4-year-old branches each year, and thin twiggy and poorly positioned growth.

Amelanchier spp.

Serviceberry, Juneberry, Saskatoon berry
ROSACEAE

Serviceberries are a great addition to the home land-scape because they are excellent shrubs and produce really good berries.

Hardiness Zones 3–8

Size 6 to 40 feet tall, 4 to 20 feet wide

Appearance These bushes are spectacular all through the year. The leaves are oval with toothed edges and turn yellow in fall. The small white or pinkish white flowers form in clusters in the spring. Berries are shiny and blue-black.

Exposure Full sun, but will tolerate partial shade in the southern reaches of their range

Soil and Water Grow in well-drained, moist soil with moderate fertility and organic matter content. They tolerate acid, rocky soils and are truly an easy-care plant except for the occasional disease outbreak.

Comments Serviceberries ripen over a period of weeks, and the average bush yields about 4 to 6 quarts of fruit, so you can generally keep up with one bush. However, if you want to preserve serviceberries, it's best to plant several bushes. Leave them widely spaced so the planting is not crowded. This will minimize diseases.

There are about 25 species of *Amelanchier* and they inter-breed easily, so you can't always be sure of getting the species you think you are. Breeders are as careful as possible, though. If you are interested in making jams and jellies, look for *A. alnifolia* 'Regent', hardy in Zones 4–9, which produces heavy crops of very sweet, blue-black fruit. Many of the serviceberries you'll find are cultivars of *A. x grandiflora,* which is a hybrid between *A. arborea* and *A. laevis.* The hybrid is known as "apple serviceberry." It grows quite large, up to 25 feet high and 30 feet. Look for its cultivar, 'Ballerina', if your roses have had fireblight because it's highly resistant to the disease. 'Strata' has branches that are quite horizontal, so it makes a striking accent plant, whether in leaf or not. The Allegheny serviceberry (*A. laevis*) grows 25 feet tall and wide. 'Cumulus', a cultivar of *A. laevis,* is usually grown as a single-stemmed tree. *A. lamarckii* is also the size of a tree, growing to a height to 30 feet and a width of 40 feet. The running serviceberry, *A. stononifera,* becomes a dense thicket of canes arising from stolons that spread in all directions. If you keep the suckers it forms under control, it can be a good addition to the landscape. The fruit is sweet and juicy, and if you don't eat it all, birds will be happy to finish the job for you.

Serviceberry (*Amelanchier* spp.)

Recommended Pruning

Season Late winter or early spring, while they are dormant

Recommended Forms Natural

Shaping Shaping is unnecessary for bush forms, although it is advisable to prune out old stems growing in the center of the plant. If you are growing 'Cumulus' and want to prune it as a tree, thin out all canes arising from the crown and all the branches on the bottom of the cane you choose as the "trunk." It will naturally grow new branches at the top of this cane, and you can choose those you want to keep and thin out the others. Head back the branches each year, always to an outward-facing bud, and thin out crowded growth that shades the interior of the plant.

Maintaining Each year, while the plant is dormant, prune out old wood. Also examine the bush for signs of damage or disease. Like all the other members of the rose family, serviceberries are susceptible to fireblight. Prune it out when you see it. However, it's often easier to see when the leaves are off the branches, so pay particular attention when you are thinning old wood. Running serviceberries must be thinned every year. Decide how large you want your thicket to be, and cut out any suckers beyond this boundary. Also thin the center of the plant to keep it productive and healthy.

Restoring Cut out old wood from the center of the bush. If it is intensely crowded, do this gradually, over the course of two or three years, so you don't shock the plant.

Ribes spp.

Red and White Currants, Gooseberries, and Jostaberries
GROSSULARIACEAE

Currants are little known in the U.S. because they are an alternate host for white pine blister rust. But if your state permits them, they make a fabulous addition to any yard.

Hardiness Zones 3 to 6

Size 3 to 5 feet tall, 3 to 5 feet wide

Appearance The leaves of *Ribes* spp. are lobed and mid-green. The flowers are small, tubular or bell-shaped, and form in clusters. Depending on the species and cultivar, they can be greenish white or a violet or purplish white. In any case, they appear very early in the spring and are not showy. Berries may be white, red, pink, or purple. The skin of gooseberries can be so transparent that you see the underlying veins, but currents are shiny and opaque.

Exposure Full sun except in hot portions of Zone 6 where filtered afternoon light is best

Red currant (*Ribes* spp.)

Recommended Pruning

Season Late winter or very early spring

Recommended Forms Bush or to a "leg" or cordon

Shaping Very little shaping is necessary if growing a bush form. Begin by cutting back all of the stems to two to four buds after planting your new bush. The following late winter or early spring, thin out weak growth; then remove all but six or seven of the strongest stems. Repeat this the following year, paying attention to the placement of the stems because the plants fruit better if they see light. If pruning to a leg, see page 94.

Maintaining In bushes, thin out the oldest stems each year and keep both the canes you kept the year before as well as three to four of the new 1-year-old canes. On legs, remove 4-year-old branches and thin the twiggy and poorly positioned growth.

Restoring Cut back plants to the ground during the dormant season. The following year, treat the plant as you did the second year after planting by choosing six or seven of the strongest canes.

Soil and Water Grow in moist, well-drained soil that is slightly acid and contains high organic matter. Spread a layer of compost around the bushes every spring, and fertilize with about 3 pounds of soybean or alfalfa meal to keep nutrients high.

Comments White pine blister rust can destroy a pine forest in a matter of years. This pathogen must spend time on both a white pine and a plant in the *Ribes* genus to survive. White pine species that are susceptible include bristlecone, limber, sugar, eastern white, southwestern white, western white, and whitebark.Of the *Ribes,* the European black currant (*R. nigrum*) is the most susceptible. As a consequence, some states have modified the law forbidding any currant or gooseberry to be grown to outlaw only black currants. And in some cases, they allow disease resistant cultivars, such as 'Consort', 'Crusader', and 'Tatiania'. Buy from a local nursery, to be sure that you are buying a cultivar that is allowed in your state.

Red currants (*R. rubrum, R. sativum,* and *R. petraeum*) actually come in many colors, including dark red, pink, yellow, white, and beige. Currents are unusual in that full coloration of the berries does not mean that they are ripe. They continue to sweeten for some time after the color is achieved. Test ripeness by picking the bottom berry from a cluster—if it is sweet, the fruit is ripe.

White currants are actually a type of red currant. The berries tend to be mild flavored and a pale yellow, rather than true white, color.

Black currants (*R. nigrum*) must be chosen for their resistance to disease. The three cultivars listed above are reliable and available even in areas where white pine grows.

Gooseberries are either American (*R. hirtellum*) or European (*R. uva-crispa*). Cultivars of the American gooseberry tend to be healthier and more productive than the European gooseberry, but the European cultivars tend to be larger and sweeter. Recommended American cultivars include 'Pixwell', a small bush that is extremely hardy (Zones 3–6) and has very small thorns.

European gooseberry cultivars include 'Invicta', which produces very high yields of large, green fruit with a somewhat bland flavor.

Sambucus canadensis

American Elderberry
CAPRIFOLIACEAE

Elderberries make excellent preserves and pies and have the added advantage of being an excellent herbal remedy for coughs, colds, flus, fevers, digestive upsets, and colic.

Hardiness Zones 2–9

Size 6 to 12 feet tall, 5 to 6 feet wide

Appearance Leaves are compound and individual leaflets are long and narrow with somewhat ruffled edges. The fragrant white flowers, which bloom in spring, droop in graceful clusters up to 10 inches wide. Berries are blue-black and shiny. In frost-free areas, elderberries can be evergreen and bloom in winter.

Exposure Full sun in Zones 2 to 5, filtered afternoon light in Zones 6 to 9

Soil and Water Grow in moist, deep, fertile, well-drained soil with high organic matter content. Fertilize with about 3 pounds of soybean or alfalfa meal each spring and spread a layer of fully finished compost under the bush.

Comments Elderberries require cross pollination with another cultivar to produce good fruit yields, so you'll need more than one plant. If you keep them pruned and in bounds, they are lovely all through the year, so this won't be a problem.

Elderberry leaves, stems, roots, and unripe fruit are mildly poisonous if you eat large quantities out of hand. You might think twice about planting them if you have a child who is prone to eating things indiscriminately. But fortunately, raw berries do not taste good, so it's rare that someone eats them, whether they are ripe or not. If you dry them, they become sweeter and more palatable.

As noted, elderberries are one of the finest herbal remedies available. You can buy tinctures and tablets at a health food store or make your own. Look for recipes for herbal oils, salves, and tinctures on the Internet. Remember that you use the leaves to make oils, salves, and tinctures and the flowers to make tea and elderwater, which is used commerically in perfumes and candies. Flower clusters, battered and fried, also make a very nice dessert.

Good cultivars include 'Aurea', a plant with golden yellow foliage and red fruit with very good flavor. The stems have a pink flush, so this plant adds drama to the landscape. 'Goldfinch' also has yellow leaves that are cut, so the plant is often used as an ornamental. 'Laciniata' has lacy cut leaves that are green rather than gold. However, it's frequently planted as an ornamental because of its leaves. 'Adams' is one of the best berry producers. The fruit are exceptionally large, but the plant does not yield

well without a pollinator. 'Johns' is commonly grown with 'Adams' because it, too, produces large, flavorful fruit that ripen earlier than those on 'Adams'. 'Kent' may be grown with 'Adams' and 'Johns', too, because the fruit size and quality are equal to theirs. It ripens early, too. 'Ebony King' produces large quantities of pitch black fruit that yield a bright red juice with excellent aroma and flavor. This is a great cultivar for wines, jellies, jams, and pies. It's also evergreen in warm climates. 'Nova' has fruit that ripen uniformly in the cluster, which is unusual, and is sweeter than many other cultivars. 'Scotia' fruit is also quite sweet and clusters also ripen uniformly. 'York' can reach 12 feet tall and produces large berries in heavy clusters. If you are looking for high productivity, include 'York' in your planting.

Recommended Pruning

Season Late winter and early spring

Recommended Forms Natural bush

Shaping Very little shaping is necessary because this plant naturally forms a lovely bush. Begin by cutting back all of the stems to two to four buds after planting. The following late winter or early spring, thin out weak growth, and then remove all but six or seven of the strongest stems. Repeat this the following year, paying attention to the placement of the stems because the plants fruit better if they see light.

Maintaining In bushes, thin out the oldest stems each year, and keep both the canes you kept the year before, as well as a few new 1-year-old canes.

Restoring Cut back plants to the ground during the dormant season. The following year, treat the plant as you did the second year after planting by choosing six or seven of the strongest canes. If you want to get rid of some of the width of the plant, dig under the unwanted portions, and either transplant them to a new area or give them to a friend.

Vaccinium angustifolium, V. ashei, V. corymbosum

Lowbush, Rabbiteye, Highbush, and Half-high Blueberries
ERICACEAE.

Blueberries are one of the easiest fruiting crops to grow as long as you can provide the acid soil and steady moisture they require.

Hardiness Zones Northern highbush: Zones 4–7, Southern highbush: Zones 7–10, Lowbush: Zones 3–8, Half-high: Zones 4–7, Rabbiteye: Zones 6–9

Size Highbush: 5 to 6 feet tall and wide; Lowbush: 1 to 3 feet tall, 5 to 8 feet wide; Half-high: 2 to 4 feet tall and wide; Rabbiteye: 15 to 18 feet tall, 5 to 6 feet wide

Appearance Leaves are glossy and dark green, sometimes with a red undertone. They have smooth margins and a pointed tip and turn red before dropping in the fall. In the south, some Southern highbush cultivars, such as 'Sebring', 'Misty', and 'Sharpblue', are evergreen rather than deciduous. Flowers are pink to creamy-white, ½ inch long, urn shaped, and waxy. They grow in clusters and open in early spring.

Highbush blueberry (*V. corymbosum*)

Exposure Full sun for half-high and high bush plants. Rabiteyes can tolerate filtered shade in the afternoon in hot climates and lowbush cultivars prefer afternoon filtered light or moderate shade in the southern reaches of their range. In the north, protect blueberries from high wind during the winter months.

Soil and Water Grow in soil with a pH between 4.5 and 5.2. Plants thrive in moist but well-drained, sandy soil and can tolerate clay soil if it contains a lot of organic matter to loosen it up. Mulch to keep roots cool and moist.

Comments Blueberries vary in their needs for chilling hours, which is one of the factors in their tolerance for various Hardiness Zones. Northern highbushes require 800–1,100 hours, while Southern highbushes require only 200–700 hours. Rabbiteyes require 350–800 hours, and lowbushes require 1,000 hours.

Blueberry blossoms are killed at 28°F, so it's often necessary to cover the bushes. They also require pollinators. Even those that are touted to be self-fruitful do far better with at least one other species growing nearby. Not only does this assure high pollination, it also spreads the picking season if you choose early, midseason, and late-bearing plants.

Blueberries are ripe from one to three days after they have turned completely blue—no red left on them. They stay good for about five days if they are left on the plant, so you can pick a couple of times a week and not lose berries.

There are literally hundreds of blueberry cultivars. Of the lowbush plants, which are most suitable for cold climates, the 12-inch-tall 'Tophat' is worth a try if you have limited space.

Half-high blueberries are crosses between lowbush and highbush berries and are extremely popular in Zones 3 and 4.

Northern highbush cultivars often bloom late and avoid frosts. Southern highbush cultivars bloom later than the Rabbiteyes grown in the region and thus escape possible late frosts.

Recommended Pruning

Season Late winter or early spring

Recommended Forms Natural

Shaping Unnecessary. But it is necessary to remove flowers for the first two years after planting so the bush can put energy into roots and shoots. Other than damaged wood, leave the bushes as they are for the first couple of years.

Maintaining For lowbush plants, cut about half of the stems to the ground every two or three years. Keep track of which part was cut so you can alternate sections each time you do this. For other types, see page 92 for directions.

Restoring When they are dormant, thin out all the old, dead, or damaged wood. You can tell that a cane is old by the bark—if it is grayish and looks as if it might peel, it is too old to be bearing well. Next, thin out all but about ten of the strongest canes. Ideally, these should be varying in age from 1 to 5 or 6 years old, but you won't be able to tell exactly. Judge age from their suppleness and the sheen of their bark.

Pruning Vines

Pruning vines to achieve the best possible health and productivity for the plant involves training them as well. Naturally, they grow up whatever support is available, usually a tree, and bear only on the topmost, sunlit branches. Yields are low, but that's fine as far as the plant is concerned, because they are certainly high enough to guarantee the survival of the species. But in the home garden, you'll want good yields and plants that remain healthy for many years. So you'll end up both training and pruning plants.

Arbors, as pictured on page 101, often seem like the easiest way to grow grape vines. And this is true, as far as pruning and training go. However, this system has some disadvantages. If you live in a marginal climate where late frosts are common, it will be hard to cover the plants on cold nights, so blossoms may be killed. The other common consequence is a high incidence of disease, particularly in humid climates. The only way around this is to get on a step ladder every year while the plant is dormant, and prune out enough growth to allow air circulation around each leaf. In dry climates, you can leave more growth without running the risk of disease. So consider carefully before growing grapes on an arbor.

Training Grapes

European, American, and hybrid grapes are usually pruned to a four-armed Kniffen system. However, if space is tight, you can also grow them as a two-armed plant, or cordon. The basic pruning is the same whether you leave four arms or two.

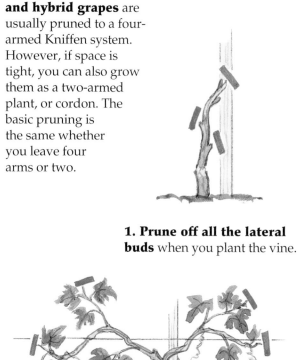

1. Prune off all the lateral buds when you plant the vine.

2. Allow two buds to develop into arms where they meet the wire.

3. Head back lateral branches that form on the shoots, and train the shoots over the wires. Allow two renewal buds to grow each year.

4. Grapes form on 1-year-old wood. Leave the shoots from which you want fruit to grow, and prune off all the others, always leaving two renewal buds.

Vaccinium agnsstifolium, V. ashei, V. cormbosum

6 Pruning Fruiting Plants

Grapes

Grapes require vigorous annual pruning and training. They require so much attention that they make a wonderful crop for people who love gardening work but a problem plant for those who do not.

The easiest and most common way to trellis European, hybrid, and American grapes is with the four-armed Kniffen system.

Set up the trellis before you plant. Use exterior-grade 4x4 or 6x6 posts, burying them below the frost line. Extend them 6 feet above the soil surface, and space them 6 to 8 feet apart from each other. Stretch 12-gauge wires from post to post at about 2 to 3 feet from the soil surface and at the top of the posts. Anchor the wires to strong stakes at each end of the trellis.

Plant each grape directly under the wire in the middle of the space between two posts. Prune back the vine to two buds near the bottom wire, and pinch off all the other buds. As the shoots develop from the two buds over the season, tie them to the wire without letting them twine around it.

The following late winter or early spring, while the plant is still dormant, select the shoot that seems the strongest and most vigorous to become the trunk of the vine. Untie it from the bottom wire, and lead it upward to the top wire. Tie it to that support. Prune off the other shoot and any lateral branches that have formed, leaving two buds near both the top and bottom wires.

Allow four buds, two at the bottom wire and two at the top, to develop during the summer, but pinch off all those that grow from the top and center portion of the trunk. Allow a renewal bud to grow on each shoot near the wire.

During the dormant period, head back the shoots, or canes, to about ten buds. During the season, grapes will grow near the bases of shoots that grow from these buds. Allow the renewal buds to develop, too, because this is where fruiting shoots will grow the following year.

In subsequent years during the dormant period, cut back the canes where fruit formed the year before, head back the current year's fruiting canes to ten buds, and allow renewal buds to remain on the plant.

Muscadine grapes are generally grown with a Munson system. This style allows greater air circulation around the foliage, making it particularly appropriate for grapes grown in the humid Southeast.

Set up a T-bar Munson trellis, as shown opposite, with posts set 6 to 8 feet apart and Ts 3 feet long. Secure the 12-gauge wire 4 feet above the soil surface and on the top surfaces at the ends of the T-bars.

Fruits growing on an overhead arbor must be harvested when ripe so that they don't drop onto the area below.

Grapes grow as well when tied to a wooden fence as on any specially made trellis.

Plant the grape under the center wire, between two posts, and cut it back to two buds. Allow these to grow during the season. While the plant is dormant, choose the shoot that will become the trunk, lead it to the wire, and tie it.

Allow two shoots to develop from the trunk, and tie them to the central wire as they grow over the summer.

During the season, shoots will grow from the arms. Drape them over the top wires. Branches that grow from these shoots will form fruit the following year. Each year, allow two new shoots to form for the following year's fruit.

If you are growing a grape over an arbor, start it off as if you were growing it as a four-armed *Kniffen* system. However, rather than allowing fruiting canes to develop low on the trunk, pinch them off in favor of those growing near the top of the vine. Each year, allow renewal buds to form near the supporting trelliswork of the arbor, and prune off all the others.

Use grapevines in the landscape by growing them on decorative arches or trellises.

Training Muscadine Grapes

Muscadine grapes are pruned and trained to a Munson system, primarily because the vines are heavy. This system allows greater air circulation, reducing the plants' vulnerability to the fungal diseases that are so prevalent in the regions where they grow.

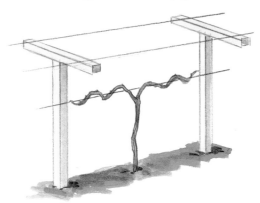

1. Prune the vine to two buds near the bottom wire after planting, and pinch off all other growth. Tie the shoots that develop to the bottom wire.

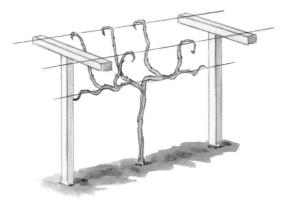

2. Drape the shoots that develop the following year over the top wires, spacing them well. Fruit will form on the laterals in the following year.

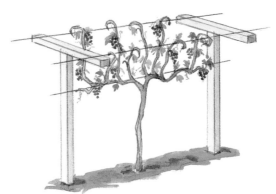

3. During the summer each year, allow two new shoots to form, and tie them to the support. Laterals growing from them will provide fruit the next year.

Vitus labrusca

American Grape
VITACEAE

These native grapes do well in the cooler, more humid areas of the country where some of the European cultivars are challenged by the weather.

Hardiness Zones 5–9

Size 12 to 15 feet long, 3 to 5 feet wide

Appearance Leaves are large and lobed with a waffle-like texture. They are a mid-green in the growing season but turn yellow before dropping in the fall. Flowers are small and inconspicuous and open in early spring.

Recommended Pruning

Season Late winter or early spring

Recommended Forms Four-armed Kniffen or arbor

Shaping When you plant, prune off all but two lateral buds that are close to the bottom wire of the trellis. (See "Training Grapes," page 99.) Over the summer, allow the two buds to develop and tie them to the bottom wire of your trellis without allowing them to twine around it. The following late winter or early spring, select the stronger of the two initial shoots to become the trunk of the vine. Untie it from the trellis, and lead it upwards to the top wire. Tie it in place. Prune off the other shoot and any laterals that have developed, leaving two buds near both the top and bottom wires. This forms your framework. Follow the directions in "Training Muscadine Grapes," on page 101 for shaping during subsequent years.

Maintaining During the dormant period, cut back the canes where fruit formed the year before, and head back the current year's fruiting canes to ten buds. Allow renewal buds to remain on the plant.

Restoring Begin by thinning the excess laterals and shoots on the vine. Head back the framework shoots, and thin out any canes where fruit has formed in previous years. Select the two strongest 1-year-old canes, and head them back to ten buds. Remove all the others, but leave renewal buds.

American grape (*Vitus labrusca*)

Exposure Full sun, preferably on a south-facing slope with good drainage and air circulation

Soil and Water Grow in deep, well-drained soil with high fertility and organic matter content. Add 1½ to 2 pounds of fully finished compost per row-foot in early spring each year. If the compost is not high quality, use more.

Comments Grapes do not need pollinators, so you can grow just one kind and get fruit. However, if you want to extend the season and also have grapes with different flavors, grow more than one. If you keep them well-pruned, they will grow well on the same trellis.

One of the best uses for American grapes, particularly the old cultivars such as Concord, is preserves. These fruits make truly excellent grape jam and jelly. They also make superb juice. If you are harvesting for jam or jelly, pick the fruit a little underripe. It contains high amounts of natural pectin, so it sets very well, and it also makes a more flavorful preserve than fully ripe fruit does.

In general, American grape cultivars have skin that slips off easily. The first 'Concord' grapes had extremely thick skin. The skin was flavorful and added texture to grape preserves, but some people found it annoying. Today, modern 'Concord' cultivars have much thinner skin, making them better for eating out of hand. You can even find seedless 'Concords', but experts recommend that you taste fruit from the parent of the plant you are planning to buy because there is some variation in flavor. In general, the intense flavor of 'Concord' grapes makes them a favorite for sweet wines and juices. This is a hardy grape that grows well in Zones 4–8. It is also quite disease resistant, which is an important quality in grapes.

'Candice' is a red, rather than a purple, cultivar. It's hardy through Zones 4–8 and ripens in mid-August. It has large clusters of very flavorful fruit and is resistant to powdery mildew and downy mildew. 'Mars' is a blue cultivar with good disease resistance. Hardy from Zones 5–8, it ripens from mid- to late August. 'Niagara' is a very popular white grape that is hardy in Zones 5–8. The fruit is big and the skin slips easily, which is an advantage for making jelly or juice. It is resistant to anthracnose and botrytis fruit rot. 'Reliance Seedless' is a red cultivar with good disease resistance. It is hardy in Zones 4–8 but, like 'Concord', ripens in September, so is not the best choice for short-season areas of Zone 4.

Vitus vinifera

European and Hybrid Grapes
VITACEAE

European grapes are the aristocrats of the family but are so susceptible to some pests and diseases that most growers prefer to grow the hybrids of European and American grapes.

Hardiness Zones 5–9

Size 12 to 20 feet long, 4 to 5 feet wide

Appearance Leaves are both lobed and toothed and have prominent veins. They are a mid-green color and turn yellow before dropping in autumn. Flowers are small and inconspicuous and open in early spring.

Exposure Full sun in an open site with good air circulation and drainage

Soil and Water Plant in deep, rich soil with high levels of organic matter. Apply about 2 pounds of compost per row foot every spring.

Comments Hybrid grapes have a great deal of historical significance. During the 1800s, the grape phylloxera aphid was destroying all the vineyards in France. But the less refined American grape was resistant to damage from the pest. When the two species were crossed, the resulting hybrids were also resistant. So it's thanks to the seedy, thick-skinned but flavorful and robust American grapes that France saved its vineyards and wineries.

There are hundreds of good hybrids and more appear every year. This is a plant that must be adapted to the climate in which it grows.

Cultivars suitable for California and Arizona are bred for their long season and low relative humidity. 'Thompson Seedless' is the most common European cultivar grown in the U.S. It's best in California and Arizona and is hardy in Zones 7 through 9. This is the white grape you see in the grocery store. It is an excellent plant that gives high yields of tight bunches. Remember that grapes don't ripen off the vine; taste the bottom grape in each cluster before you cut it.

'Black Monukka' is a good dark red cultivar in both California and Arizona as well as in the Southeastern U.S. 'Olivette Blanche' is a green seedless cultivar grown in California and Arizona.

'Himrod' was bred at Cornell's Geneva, New York experiment station and is an excellent grape for the humid northeast. Pick bunches as soon as they are ripe because grapes drop if they are left for more than a day or two.

'Interlaken Seedless' is literally a sibling of 'Himrod' because it was bred from the same parents. It, too, is green and seedless, but it ripens a week earlier and

Hybrid grapes (*Vitus vinifera*)

yields up to 30 pounds per plant. If you live in Zones 5-8, consider this grape.

'Lakemont' is another Eastern grape. The skin on the small to medium, seedless, white grapes is firmly attached to the flesh, and the honey-flavored grapes are crisp to the bite. The vines are lovely.

Recommended Pruning

Season Late winter or early spring

Recommended Forms Four-armed Kniffen or arbor

Shaping When you plant, prune off all but two lateral buds that are close to the bottom wire of the trellis. (See "Training Grapes," page 99.) Over the summer, allow the two buds to develop, and tie them to the bottom wire of your trellis without allowing them to twine around it. The following late winter or early spring, select the stronger of the two initial shoots to become the trunk of the vine. Untie it from the trellis, and lead it upwards to the top wire. Tie it in place. Prune off the other shoot and any laterals that have developed, leaving two buds near both the top and bottom wires. This forms your framework. Follow the directions in "Training Muscadine Grapes," on page 101 for shaping during subsequent years.

Maintaining During the dormant period, cut back the canes where fruit formed the year before, and head back the current year's fruiting canes to ten buds. Allow renewal buds to remain on the plant.

Restoring Begin by thinning the excess laterals and shoots on the vine. Head back the framework shoots, and thin out any canes where fruit has formed in previous years. Select the two strongest 1-year old canes, and head them back to 10 buds. Remove all the others, but leave renewal buds.

Vitus rotundifolia

Muscadine, Scuppernong
VITACEAE

This large grape is a favorite in the Southern areas where it grows.

Hardiness Zones 7–10

Size 12 to 20 feet tall, 3 to 5 feet wide

Appearance The leaves are toothed but not lobed and a bluish green color. They turn yellow in fall before dropping. Flowers are tiny, greenish, and borne in inconspicuous clusters in spring.

Exposure Full sun

Soil and Water Plant in rich, well-drained soil with abundant organic matter. Add an inch or so of compost around the roots each spring, just before growth resumes.

Comments Some cultivars require pollinators, so check with your supplier when you buy. If you do get two cultivars, you can be assured of high yields of fruit, ideally coming in at slightly different times in the season.

Recommended cultivars include 'Carlos', which has slightly smaller fruit than some other cultivars but is self-fertile. It's a "bronze" muscadine, meaning that it is gold with a pink flush. The plant is very disease-resistant, so it's a good grape if you are in a spot with low wind and air circulation. It's recommended for preserves, too, so if grape jelly is one of your motivations for growing grapes, this is a good cultivar for you.

'Hunt' has dull black fruit and is also very disease-resistant. It's frequently used as a pollinator for other cultivars.

'Magoon' is a self-fertile plant that produces high yields of redish purple, medium size grapes that are highly aromatic.

'Scuppernong' vines may produce green or red-bronze fruits. The grapes

Scuppernong
(*Vitus rotundifolia*)

are very sweet and juicy. It requires a pollinator and is often grown with 'Hunt'.

'Southland' is recommended for Florida because it can stand up to the very high humidity and drenching summer rains. It is a self-fertile plant that produces large, purple, very sweet fruit.

Recommended Pruning

Season Late winter or early spring

Recommended Forms Munson system pruning and training

Shaping After planting, if the vine is already long enough to reach the bottom wire, prune it to two buds near the wire, and pinch off all other growth. If it is not this tall, train it up a piece of nylon twine tied to the wire. When it reaches the wire, cut it back to about 4 inches below the wire to encourage "V"-shaped branching, taking care that there are two buds near the cut. In either case, with an already tall vine or one you let grow, the next step is to tie the shoots that grow from the two buds to the wire, so that they face in different directions. Make sure that the shoots don't wrap around the wire because you'll need to release them without injury. Continue to prune off all the laterals that try to grow from the trunk. In late winter the following year, choose the shoot that will become the trunk, lead it to the wire, and tie it to the wire. Prune off the other shoot. During the growing season, allow two shoots to develop from the trunk, and tie them to the wire. The following late winter, head back the shoots, which have now hardened up to become the "arms" of your grapevine, and allow two buds to remain on the plant to grow during the season. Head back all other growth. Shoots will now grow from the two arms. As they do, drape them over the top wires. Fruiting wood will develop from these shoots.

Maintaining Each year, remove the old fruiting wood, and allow two new arms to form. Shoots growing from them will be your fruiting wood.

Restoring Cut out most of the permanent arms, leaving only 6-inch stubs. New shoots will arise from the stubs over the season. Choose the two you will retain, and tie them to the wire. Remove all the other growth. Allow these shoots to develop over the season, and head them back slightly in late winter. New fruiting shoots will develop over the next season and you'll be back in grapes the following year.

Actinidia deliciosa, A. arguta, A. kolomikta

Kiwifruti, Hardy Kiwifruit
ACTINIDIACEAE

Kiwifruit are a real treat. In California, you can grow the type sold in the grocery store, but in cold regions, the hardy kiwifruit thrives.

Hardiness Zones *A. deliciosa,* Zones 7–10; *A. arguta* and *A. kolomikta,* Zones 4–9

Size 15 to 39 feet long, 3 to 5 feet wide

Appearance Leaves are bronze or reddish green when young and turn dark green and shiny as they mature. They are oval and have deep veins and slightly toothed margins. Male *A. kolomikta* plants have variegated leaves that are green, cream, and pink. Flowers are cream colored, cup-shaped, and fragrant in some cultivars, and plants bear either male or female blooms.

Exposure Full sun for *A. deliciosa.* North of Zone 7, kiwifruit fare best if they grow on a north-facing slope in partial shade to protect them from winter injury.

Soil and Water Plant in well-drained soil with high fertility and organic matter levels with a pH between 5.0 and 6.5. These are heavy feeders and may need supplemental balanced fertilizers in addition to a yearly mulch of 2 inches of fully finished compost.

Comments *A. deliciosa* is the egg-shaped, fuzzy, brown kiwifruit you probably associate with the name "kiwi." 'Hayward' is the predominant commercial variety in California. It has excellent flavor. Home gardeners can keep just harvested fruit for as long as two months, but when it's fully ripe, it keeps only a week in the refrigerator. It requires about 800 chilling hours to break dormancy. 'Chico' is the most common pollinator for 'Hayward', although 'Matua' and 'Tomori' are also appropriate.

In areas that don't have 800 chilling hours, cultivars such as 'Elmwood', 'Dexter', 'Abbott', or 'Vincent' are better choices. In years when the weather is especially mild, the plants often retain their leaves and they may not flower or fruit the following season.

Both types of hardy kiwifruit, *A. arguta,* and *A. kolomikta,* are about the size of a grape or cherry. They are the greenish yellow inside and have black seeds, but their skins are smooth and edible. Pick them when they are ripe or close to it because they will not ripen until the seeds have turned black. Unripe fruit are quite acidic. Of the two, *A. kolomikta* has the smaller fruit and is hardier. It survives temperatures of -30°F in comparison to the -20–25°F that *A. arguta* survives. Their fruit has an extremely high content of vitamin C.

Kiwifruit
(*A. deliciosa*)

Recommended Pruning

Season Both late winter or early spring and summer

Recommended Forms Pruned and trained to a T-bar

Shaping After planting, choose the strongest shoot to become the trunk of the vine. Remove all sideshoots. Continue to remove laterals all season. Trellis on two levels of wires.

When the trunk reaches the wire, train it along the wire. Leave a renewal bud close to the place where the trunk makes the bend. This will produce a shoot that can be trained along the wire in the opposite direction. These two shoots become the permanent framework of the vine. Do not let them twist around the wire. Once they have extended the length of the wire, head them back in late winter and allow lateral shoots to develop. Tie the laterals to the upper wires so they are perpendicular to the arms and thin them to 8 to 12 inches apart while the plant is dormant. Buds for both flowers and vegetative growth will develop in the leaf axils of these side branches.

Maintaining Summer pruning is done just before the plants flower to remove excessive growth. Remove nonflowering shoots that are growing outside the wires and cut back the flowering shoots four to six leaves past the last flower. Remove poorly positioned shoots. Later in the summer, remove any shoots that are not needed for replacement, and head back the replacement shoots.

During winter or early spring pruning, cut back shoots that are less than a pencil width in diameter and all the wood that fruited the previous year. New fruiting wood develops at the base of the previous year's canes.

Prune male plants immediately after flowering. Do not prune male plants during the dormant season.

Restoring Follow the directions for Muscadine grapes.

6 Pruning Fruiting Plants

Pruning Brambles

All bramble fruit—raspberries, blackberries, loganberries, dewberries, boysenberries, and more—require pruning and training to maintain good health and reach their potential productivity. Without exception, they grow best on a trellis.

The three most common types of trellises for brambles include the T-bar trellis, the double-post-and-wire trellis, and the cable-and-post-fence support. Each of these supports can be used for any of the erect or semierect cultivars, but the cable-and-post-fence support is the most practical for the long canes of trailing blackberries.

Set up the trellis you plan to use before planting the berries. Spring planting, while the plants are still dormant, is generally recommended for bare-root plants in Zone 5 and northward. In Zone 6 and southward, plant while the canes are dormant in the spring or in the fall, at least a month before the ground freezes.

Plant the berry bushes slightly deeper than they were growing at the nursery. Space them as recommended on the following page. If the tip of a cane looks damaged, head it back until you reach healthy tissue. Head back undamaged canes to a length of 6 inches to stimulate new growth.

During the first year, summer-bearing cultivars will produce a healthy crop of primocanes—the stems that will become fruiting floricanes the following year. The fall-bearers will also produce primocanes, some of which may produce a small crop of berries the first year.

Depending on the type of trellis you have set up, your job during the first year will be to move the canes into position between or against the wires and tie them in place. Keep up with this throughout the season so that your fall work is minimal.

During the dormant season, thin the canes if they are growing more closely together than 6 inches, and head back the remaining canes. If you are growing a trailing blackberry, it is best to wrap the long canes around the top wire and head them back only a few inches. Head back the shorter, erect cultivars so that they are only a foot above the top wire.

There are two ways to handle the plants during the summer. You can tie the new primocanes to the bottom wire of your support until after the the floricanes are harvested, or you can divide the planting so that all the floricanes are trained to one side and all the primocanes to the other. Separating the canes in this way may seem like extra work, but it saves time and trouble in the long run, especially when you are picking and pruning old floricanes.

After Fruiting. Once the floricanes have fruited, they will die. If you simply leave them in the plant, they inhibit air movement and provide a niche for some pests. Many gardeners suggest leaving them in place until late winter, but it is often preferable to prune them out in the fall. For one thing, they are easy to spot, and for another, you can open up the planting so that it is easier to mulch. But no matter when you thin, make all the cuts just above the soil surface. For sanitation's sake, remove the old canes from the area, and do not compost them. Once all the old wood has been removed, retie the primocanes. If you are doing this work during the dormant period, thin and head back the remaining canes as described above. However, if you prune out old wood in the fall, wait until late winter to thin and head back or you may encourage new, vulnerable growth.

Fall-bearers are sometimes pruned differently. If the canes have developed diseases or the planting has been neglected and is now too crowded, you have the option of cutting all the canes to the ground. If you plan to do this, you can prune in late fall, after the canes have become dormant, or wait until late winter. The plant will flower and fruit on the tips of the primocanes the following spring, and you'll have a chance to make the planting more manageable.

Wire supports allow you to work with the plants from both sides and also provide excellent air circulation.

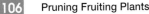

Rubus spp.

Raspberry, Blackberry, Boysenberry, Dewberry, Loganberry, Tayberry
ROSACEAE

Brambles can be truly multipurpose in your yard, serving as both a fence and a source of delicious and nutritious berries.

Hardiness Zones Blackberry, Dewberry, and Loganberry, 5–10; Boysenberry, 6–8; Raspberry, 3–9

Size Erect cultivars: 5 to 10 feet long, 3 to 5 feet wide; Trailing plants: 15 to 18 feet long, 4 to 5 feet wide

Appearance Leaves of bramble fruit are a dull green with deep veins. They have three leaflets and toothed margins. In fall, they turn a dusty red color. Flowers form in clusters and are white or pink, an inch wide, and have the characteristic prominent center of all rose family blooms.

Exposure Full sun. Protect from strong winds in Zones 6 and cooler, but site them so that air passes through them.

Soil and Water Deep, well-drained, moist soils with average fertility and high organic matter. Like all fruits, brambles thrive with a yearly application of compost over their roots. For maximum sugar content, do not supplement natural rainfall, unless there is a drought and the soil is really dry, from the time the fruit begins to color until it is harvested.

Comments Brambles are truly gratifying. For very little work, and a time investment of only a year, you can have huge crops of delicious fruit. Blackberries can be upright or erect, or trailing. In general, thornless types are trailing, so you'll need wrap their long canes around the top wire of your trellis. As always, choose a cultivar that does well in your region.

Raspberries may be summer or fall bearing. The fall

Raspberries (*Rubus* spp.)   **Blackberry** 'thornfree'

bearing plants also fruit in the early summer, although yields are generally not as good as they are in the fall. Among the summer-bearing plants, there is still variation in harvest times. 'Boyne' is a good choice for the early crop. The fruit is soft and small to medium but has good flavor and yields well. It is especially recommended for cold areas in Zone 5 and most spots in Zone 4. 'Bristol' is a summer-bearing black raspberry with excellent flavor that yields in midseason. Of all the purple raspberries, 'Royalty' is generally considered the best. The plants are vigorous and extremely productive. It's also unattractive to aphids, so it doesn't contract some of the virus diseases that plague other brambles. The fruit is large, sweet, and flavorful. 'Heritage' is the most widely planted fall-bearing raspberry because of its disease resistance, high yields, firmness, and excellent flavor. It ripens late, toward the end of September.

Loganberries are not the best tasting of the brambles. They are, however, an excellent parent to various crosses, such as tayberries. These resemble blackberries in flavor and fragrance, ripen earlier than blackberries, and are quite soft. This softness prevents their being a good commercial crop. 'Buckingham' is nearly thornless, making it easier to harvest.

Boysenberries are a cross between loganberry and dewberry according to some people, and a cross between raspberry and blackberry according to others. This is a trailing, almost thornless plant that ripens early and has high yields.

Dewberries native to this country are small plants that trail along the ground, rooting at the nodes. In Europe, they were bred to be erect plants and these are now available in some parts of this country. The fruit is very soft, making it impossible to ship well, but it's very sweet. It is usually purple or black and has a hint of black raspberry flavor. The European dewberry has a "dew" of waxy droplets on the skin of the fruit, making it look blue. Even though it is easier to pick, it lacks the good flavor of the native, ground-hugging plant.

Recommended Pruning

Season Late winter and early spring, or fall

Recommended Forms Trellised and supported

Shaping After planting, head back to 6 inches above the ground.

Maintaining See "Pruning Brambles," opposite, for instructions.

Restoring Cut canes to the ground; let them regrow.

zone maps

Average Annual Minimum Temperature

Temp. (°C)	Zone	Temp. (°F)
−45.6 & below	1	below −50
−42.8 to −45.5	2a	−45 to −50
−40.0 to −42.7	2b	−40 to −45
−37.3 to −40.0	3a	−35 to −40
−34.5 to −37.2	3b	−30 to −35
−31.7 to −34.4	4a	−25 to −30
−28.9 to −31.6	4b	−20 to −25
−26.2 to −28.8	5a	−15 to −20
−23.4 to −26.1	5b	−10 to −15
−20.6 to −23.3	6a	−5 to −10
−17.8 to −20.5	6b	0 to −5
−15.0 to −17.7	7a	5 to 0
−12.3 to −15.0	7b	10 to 5
−9.5 to −12.2	8a	15 to 10
−6.7 to −9.4	8b	20 to 15
−3.9 to −6.6	9a	25 to 20
−1.2 to −3.6	9b	30 to 25
1.6 to −1.1	10a	35 to 30
4.4 to 1.7	10b	40 to 35
4.5 & above	11	40 & above

The USDA Hardiness Map divides North America into 11 zones according to average minimum winter temperatures. Hardiness zones are used to identify regions to which plants are suited based on their cold tolerance, which is what "hardiness" means. Many factors, such as elevation and moisture level, come into play when determining whether a plant is suitable for your region. Local climates may vary from what is shown on this map. Contact your local Cooperative Extension Service for recommendations for your area.

Plant Hardiness Zones

0a	4a
0b	4b
1a	5a
1b	5b
2a	6a
2b	6b
3a	7a
3b	7b
	8a

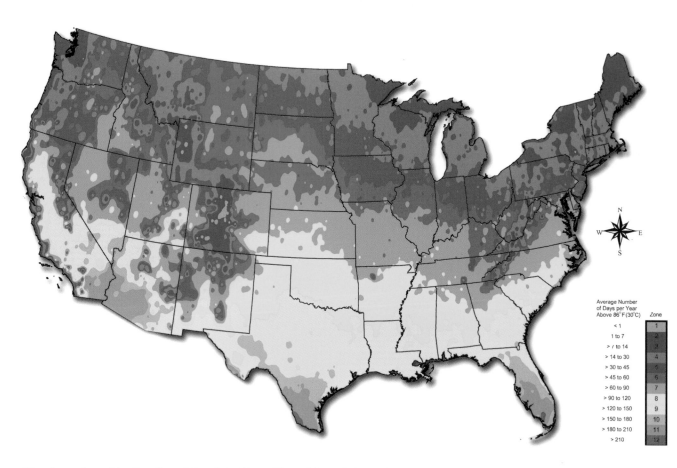

Average Number of Days per Year Above 86°F (30°C)	Zone
< 1	1
1 to 7	2
> 7 to 14	3
> 14 to 30	4
> 30 to 45	5
> 45 to 60	6
> 60 to 90	7
> 90 to 120	8
> 120 to 150	9
> 150 to 180	10
> 180 to 210	11
> 210	12

The American Horticultural Society Heat-Zone Map divides the United States into 12 zones based on the average annual number of days a region's temperatures climb above 86°F (30°C), the temperature at which the cellular proteins of plants begin to experience injury. Introduced in 1998, the AHS Heat-Zone Map holds significance, especially for gardeners in southern and transitional zones. Nurseries, growers, and other plant sources will gradually begin listing both cold hardiness and heat tolerance zones for plants, including grass plants. Using the USDA Plant Hardiness map, which can help determine a plant's cold tolerance, and the AHS Heat-Zone Map, gardeners will be able to safely choose plants that tolerate their region's lowest and highest temperatures.

Canada's Plant Hardiness Zone Map outlines the different zones in Canada where various types of trees, shrubs, and flowers will most likely survive. It is based on the average climatic conditions of each area. The hardiness map is divided into nine major zones: the harshest is 0 and the mildest is 8. Relatively few plants are suited to zone 0. Subzones (e.g., 4a or 4b, 5a or 5b) are also noted in the map legend. These subzones are most familiar to Canadian gardeners. Some significant local factors, such as micro-topography, amount of shelter, and subtle local variations in snow cover, are too small to be captured on the map. Year-to-year variations in weather and gardening techniques can also have a significant impact on plant survival in any particular location.

glossary

Alternate Alternate leaf placement, rather than opposite or in a whirl, on a stem.

Annual A plant that germinates, grows, flowers, produces seeds, and dies in the course of a single growing season.

Anther The endmost part of a flower stamen where pollen is produced.

Antitranspirant A substance sprayed on the stems and leaves to slow transpiration (water loss) resulting from drying winter winds.

Axil The angle where a leaf joins a stem.

Bare-root A plant dug out of the ground and then shaken or washed at its roots to remove the soil.

Bract A modified leaf or leaflike structure that embraces a flower bud and opens with the flower. Bracts occur at the base of the flower and may be part of the flower head.

Catkin A drooping spike of many small flowers, common on wind-pollinated trees.

Compound leaf A leaf with two or more leaflets branching off a single stalk.

Conifer A usually evergreen woody plant bearing conelike fruit and needlelike leaves.

Container-grown A plant raised in a container that is removed before planting.

Crown Where roots and stem meet, usually at soil level. It is also the term for the canopy, or "upper story," of a tree.

Cultivar Short for cultivated variety. A plant variety developed in cultivation, rather than occurring naturally in the wild.

Cutting A part of a plant (often a stem section) removed and planted in order to grow a new plant.

Deadheading Removing spent flowers during the growing season to prevent seed formation and to encourage new flowers.

Deciduous A tree, shrub, or vine that drops all of its leaves in fall or winter.

Dioecious Plants that bear male and female flowers on separate plants. See *Monoecious*.

Division Propagation of a plant by separating it into two or more pieces, each of which has at least one bud and some roots.

Double flower A flower with more than the standard number of rows of petals.

Evergreen Either a broad-leaved plant or a conifer that retains foliage for at least a year.

Floret A small flower in a multiflowered flower head.

Foundation plantings Woody plants that form the main features, or the "structure," in a landscape; also a narrow border of evergreen shrubs along the foundation of a house.

Genus (plural: genera) A closely related group of species sharing similar characteristics and probably evolved from the same ancestors. In scientific, or botanical, language the genus name begins with a capital letter and is followed by the species name, which begins with a lowercase letter. Both words are italicized, as in *Acer palmatum*.

Habit The characteristic shape or form a plant assumes as it grows.

Hardiness A plant's ability to survive winter cold or summer heat without protection.

Hardiness zone A geographic region where the coldest temperature in an average winter falls within a certain range, such as between 0° and –10°F.

Hard pruning Cutting away most of a shrub's top growth, leaving just stubs.

Humus Fibrous residues of decomposing organic materials in soil. Humus absorbs moisture and is an essential element of good garden soil.

Hybrid A plant resulting from cross breeding plants that belong to different varieties, species, or genera. Hybrids are indicated in scientific names by a times sign (x) between the genus and species name, as in red horse chestnut (*Aesculus* x *carnea* 'Briotii').

Invasive plant A plant that spreads quickly, usually by runners, and mixes with or dominates adjacent plantings.

Leaflet One segment of a compound leaf.

Loam Natural or amended soil that is well-structured, fertile, moisture-retentive, and free draining. Loam contains a balanced mix of sand, silt, and clay particles, as well as organic matter.

Monoecious A plant that bears both male and female flowers. See *Dioecious*.

Naturalized A plant introduced to an area that has escaped cultivation and reproduces on its own.

New wood Stems and branches that have grown during the current season.

Nutrients Nitrogen, phosphorus, potassium, calcium, magnesium, sulfur, iron, and other elements needed by growing plants.

Old wood Stems and branches that developed during a previous growing season.

Panicle A loose, branched flower cluster on which the flowers bloom gradually from bottom to top or from the center outward.

Perennial A plant that lives for a number of years, generally flowering each year.

Pistil The female, central, part of a flower. See *Anther*.

Raceme A spikelike stalk with numerous flowers on individual stems.

Rootball The mass of soil and roots dug up with a plant when it is removed from the ground or from a container.

Single flower A flower with a single concentric row of petals.

Species Among plants, a group that shares many characteristics, including essential flower characteristics, and can interbreed freely. In scientific, or botanical, language the species name always follows the genus name and begins with a lowercase letter, and both words are italicized, as in *Abies concolor*.

Specimen plant A plant that is featured in a prominent position.

Spike An elongated flower cluster, with individual flowers borne on short stalks or attached directly to the main stem.

Stamen One of the male reproductive organs of a flower, consisting of an anther (which produces pollen) supported by a stalklike filament. See *Anther*.

Standard A plant trained to grow a round bushy head of branches atop a single upright trunk.

Watersprout A shoot that grows almost vertically from a relatively horizontal branch.

index

Glossary/Index

index

photo credits

GHP= Grant Heilman Photography, Inc., DPA= Dembinsky Photo Associates, GPL= The Garden Picture Library

page 1: Nick Johnson/Positive Images **page 3:** *all* Jerry Pavia **page 4:** *left* Neil Soderstrom *center* David Cavagnaro *right* Crandall & Crandall **page 5:** *top* Joseph G. Strauch, Jr. *bottom* Lefever/Grushow/GHP **page 6:** *top left* Jerry Pavia *top right* Derek Fell *bottom* Lefever/Grushow/GHP **page 7:** Lamontagne/GPL **page 11:** Neil Soderstrom **page 13:** Jerry Pavia **page 14:** *top left* Nick Johnson/Positive Images *top right* and *bottom left* Susan A. Roth *bottom right* Richard Shiell/DPA **page 15:** David Cavagnaro **page 16:** *both left* Neil Soderstrom *right* Michael & Lois Warren/Photos Horticultural **page 18:** *left* Lefever/Grushow/GHP *right* Derek Fell **page 19:** *left* Susan A. Roth *right* John Glover **page 20:** *top left* Susan A. Roth *bottom left* Neil Soderstrom/Rosedale Nurseries *right* Derek Fell **page 21:** *top* and *center* Michael Dirr *bottom* Richard Shiell/DPA **page 22:** *left* Christi Carter/GHP *top right* Janet Loughrey *bottom right* Susan A. Roth **page 23:** *left* Michael Dirr *top right* Susan A. Roth *bottom right* Susan A. Roth **page 24:** *bottom left* Susan A. Roth *bottom right* Richard Shiell/DPA *top right* Michael Dirr *center right* Derek Fell **page 25:** *top left* courtesy of Monrovia Nurseries *bottom left* and *top right* Michael Dirr *bottom right* David Cavagnaro **page 26:** *left* Michael Dirr *top left* Susan A. Roth *top* and *bottom right* Jerry Pavia **page 27:** *top* Derek Fell *center* Susan A. Roth *bottom* Jim Strawser/GHP **page 28:** *left* Jane Grushow/GHP *top right* Derek Fell *left center* Jerry Pavia *right center* Jane Grushow/GHP **page 29:** *both left* Susan A. Roth *right* Jerry Pavia **page 30:** *left* Susan A. Roth *center* Michael Dirr *right* Joseph G. Strauch, Jr. **page 31:** *left* Derek Fell *top right* Joseph G. Strauch, Jr. *left center* Michael Dirr *right center* Richard Shiell/DPA **page 32:** *top left* Alan *and* Linda Detrick *top right* Derek Fell *bottom left* David Cavagnaro *bottom right* Friedrich Strauss/GPL **page 33:** *left* Neil Soderstrom *right* Linda Burgess/GPL **page 35:** Derek Fell **page 36:** *top* David Askham/GPL *bottom* Walter Chandoha **page 37:** both Neil Soderstrom **page 38:** *top* Derek Fell *bottom* Neil Soderstrom **page 39:** *top left* Jerry Pavia *top right* Alan and Linda Detrick *bottom right* Ron Evans/GPL **page 40:** *top left* Michael Dirr *top right* David Cavagnaro *bottom left* Jerry Pavia *bottom right* Walter Chandoha **page 43:** *top right* Rick Mastelli *all others* Michael Dirr **page 44:** *top* Michael Dirr *center* Christi Carter/GHP *bottom* Neil Soderstrom **page 45:** *left* Richard Shiell/DPA *top right* Lefever/Grushow/GHP *bottom right* Lefever/Grushow/GHP **page 46:** both Michael Dirr **page 47:** *left* Michael Dirr *top right* Susan A. Roth *bottom right* Richard Shiell/DPA **page 48:** *top* and *center* Michael & Lois Warren/Photos Horticultural *bottom* Jim Strawser/GHP **page 49:** *top* Matthew J. Vehr *bottom left* John Glover *bottom center* Jerry Pavia *bottom right*

Richard Shiell/DPA **page 50:** *top* David Cavagnaro *center* John Glover *bottom* Jim Strawser/GHP **page 51:** *all* Michael Dirr **page 52:** *top* Neil Soderstrom, White Flower Farm *center* Joseph G. Strauch, Jr. *bottom* Janet Loughrey **page 53:** *top and bottom left* Susan A. Roth *top right* Richard Shiell/DPA *center* Jerry Pavia **page 54:** *top left* Susan A. Roth *top right and bottom left* Michael Dirr *bottom left* Neil Soderstrom, Institute of Ecosystem Studies, Mary Flaglar Cary **page 55:** Walter Chandoha **page 58:** *all* Walter Chandoha **pages 60–61:** *all* Neil Soderstrom **page 62:** *top* Neil Soderstrom, Hollandia Nursery and Garden Center *bottom left* Michael Dirr *bottom right* Neil Soderstrom, Institute of Ecosystem Studies, Mary Flaglar Cary **page 63:** *top* Susan A. Roth *bottom left* Runk/Schoenberger/GHP *bottom right* Neil Soderstrom, Pepsico World Headquarters **page 64:** *both left* Jerry Pavia *right* Michael Dirr **page 65:** *bottom left* John Glover *bottom right* Michael Dirr *top* Virginia Weinland *center left* John Colwell/GHP *center right* Jim Strawser/GHP **page 66:** *top* Michael Dirr *center* Jerry Pavia *bottom* Jane Grushow/GHP **page 67:** *both left* Michael Dirr *right* Susan A. Roth **page 68:** *left and bottom right* Michael Dirr *top right* Jerry Pavia *center* Michael Dirr *bottom* Susan A. Roth **page 70:** *all* Michael Dirr **page 71:** *left and center* Jerry Pavia *right* Michael Dirr **page 72:** *top and bottom right* Michael Dirr *bottom left* Jerry Pavia **page 73:** *left and right* Michael Dirr *center* Richard Shiell/DPA **page 74:** *top* Larry Lefever/GHP *inset and bottom left* Susan A. Roth *bottom right* Jerry Pavia **page 75:** *top* Michael Dirr *bottom left* Susan A. Roth *bottom right* Derek Fell **page 76:** *top* Susan A. Roth *center and bottom* Neil Soderstrom **page 77:** *top* Neil Soderstrom, Vassar Arboretum *bottom left* Michael Dirr *bottom right* Neil Soderstrom **page 78:** *top* Susan A. Roth *bottom left* Michael Dirr *bottom right* Neil Soderstrom **page 79:** *top left* Joseph G. Strauch, Jr. *top right* Michael Dirr *bottom left* David Cavagnaro *bottom right* Richard Shiell/DPA **page 80:** *top left* Neil Holmes/GPL *top center* Jerry Pavia *top right* H. Lange/Okapia/Photo Researchers *bottom* Mayer/Le Scanff/GPL **page 81:** Walter Chandoha **page 83:** *both* Walter Chandoha **page 84:** *left* Photos Horticultural *right* Walter Chandoha **page 85:** *top* Crandall & Crandall *bottom* Derek Fell **page 86:** *left* Lamontagne/GPL *right* Michael Thompson **page 87:** Jerry Pavia **page 88:** John Glover **page 89:** H. Lange/Okapia/Photo Researchers **page 90:** W. Weisser/Bruce Coleman **page 91:** Jerry Pavia **page 92:** Photos Horticultural **page 95:** Erwin and Peggy Bauer/Bruce Coleman Inc. **page 96:** Walter Chandoha **page 97:** Gilbert Grant/Photo Researchers, Inc. **page 98:** Jerry Pavia **page 100:** *left* Photos Horticultural *right* Walter Chandoha **page 101:** Derek Fell **page 102:** Walter Chandoha **page 103:** L & D Klein/Photo Researchers, Inc. **page 104:** Neil Holmes/GPL **page 105:** Photos Horticultural **pages 106–107:** *all* David Cavagnaro